THE YOUNG CIVILIAN

THE YOUNG
CIVILIAN
A GLASGOW WARTIME BOYHOOD
BOB CRAMPSEY

MAINSTREAM
PUBLISHING

First published in Great Britain in 1987 by
MAINSTREAM PUBLISHING COMPANY (EDINBURGH) LTD
7 Albany Street
Edinburgh EH1 3UG

ISBN 1 85158 076 X (cloth)

British Library Cataloguing in Publication Data

Crampsey, Robert A.
    The young civilian: a Glasgow wartime boyhood.
    1. World War, 1939-1945—Personal narratives, Scottish.
    2. World War, 1939-1945—Social aspects—Scotland—Glasgow (Strathclyde)
    3. Glasgow (Strathclyde)—Social life and customs.
    I. Title
    941.4'43'0840924   D811.5
    ISBN 1 85158 076 X

Typeset by Mainstream Publishing, Edinburgh.
Printed in Great Britain by Garden City Press, Letchworth.

The author and the publishers are grateful to George Outram & Co. Ltd., for their kind co-operation in providing much of the photographic material in this book.

*To the Glasgow parents of 1939 who brought
their children through to 1945.*

Contents

Foreword

This book does not in any sense claim to be the definitive Glasgow civilian experience of World War 2. For a start, there was no such thing and my own experience was certainly untypical in that, because of the age composition of my family, there was no one closely related to me serving with the Forces. We were therefore mercifully free of the numbing fear which was always at the back of the minds of those whose close relatives were away on service.

Wars are times of extraordinary occurrences and homeric deeds and there were plenty of those. There was also a marvellous normality in many areas as things continued to function well under great stress and perhaps the newspapers exemplify this best. As the paper ration was cut back they shrank ruthlessly in size until the twenty-page publication at the outbreak of war had become one of four pages five years later. The delivery vans which had been a feature of peace-time soon went off the road and for most of the time I delivered newspapers they arrived at the local station by suburban train. Yet arrive they did and in the amount of information given and in their typographical layout, no matter that latterly they were produced by the proverbial four old men and two boys, they were an object lesson to some of their contemporary descendants.

It was not a period of universal sweetness and light. It was not a period of light at all, the grim unrelenting darkness has got to be the most graphic memory of the conflict. Nor was everyone in the shopping queue the Scottish equivalent of Mrs Miniver; irritation and fatigue were cumulative things and there was a great weariness by 1944, even if largely unexpressed, perhaps even unrealised.

For children, it was a strange time. We were increasingly without the pleasant things of life, a deprivation the more keenly felt in that we were just old enough to have some memory of them. And yet it was a wonderful time in which to grow up; it was impossible not to be conscious of the titanic events that were taking place all around.

We learned that it is possible, for some strange reason, to be unafraid in times of considerable physical danger, not always and not in response to every kind of physical danger, but sometimes. We came to learn, horrified and unwillingly, that whereas occupation by the Germans would be hard and inconvenient for such as us, it would mean extermination for some families we knew and for some children with whom we played.

There was comparatively little rational thinking about the war. I thought that then and I think it now. This was not a fault, rational thinking about the war would have led to a surrender in 1940 and even perhaps as late as 1942 to a negotiated peace.

The burdens of the war were shared as equitably as they could be in an imperfect human society. The service personnel had the danger and tremendous sufferings in certain times and places but they also had the excitement and they were much better fed. For the first time ever civilians at home were liable to be killed and indeed for a few months in late 1940 and early 1941 were being killed in greater numbers than those in the Forces.

The heroes and heroines of this book are the forty-year-olds who perforce had to stay at home. The men worked long hours in munitions factories or tried to run businesses when Government intervention made commerce a nightmare and when the younger partners or employees had gone off to the colours. When they had coped with the day-to-day demands of business there was the Home Guard waiting or duty as an Air Raid Warden or a spot of fire-watching to be done.

The wives and mothers had to feed their households from resources which steadily dwindled in both quantity and variety and to keep the home functioning in the face of a hundred and one shortages, and it was often the more apparently trivial ones which were the most exasperating and depressing. The parents of the children of my time had an unremitting and undramatic task, the harder because no definite term could be assigned to it. For six years, while the days were grey and the nights black, and in an atmosphere which had none of the exhilarating hysteria of the First World War, they strove to see that their children had as normal an upbringing as possible. They were astonishingly successful and their success is abundantly worth commemorating.

NOTE: Some readers may on occasion quarrel with the words of songs as they are here set down. I have tended to write them down as I remember singing them or listening to them and in my defence I will cite G K Chesterton who declared that where he misquoted, he improved.

Chapter One

A Glasgow wartime boyhood

EARLY on Sunday morning, 9 July 1939, the *Lairdsburn* nosed slowly up the River Foyle and docked in Derry. In addition to her holidaymakers and the miscellaneous cargo which the Derry boat always carried, she was bearing my father and my younger brothers, Frank and Phil. We were not holiday-making in the strict sense. My mother who had been unwell since the birth of my sister Julie in November 1938, a girl welcomed much more rapturously by the adult members of the family than by her brothers at the time, was about to undergo an operation for the removal of a kidney and it was imperative that we boys should be cleared out of the way to my father's people in Ireland. My mother and Julie had accompanied us to the dock in Glasgow and it would be nice to say that we parted in sorrow but we did not. We parted with the callous incomprehension of youth and as the gap widened between ship and quay our thoughts were almost exclusively on what lay ahead. We had no thoughts of parental worries or misgivings—none at all.

Indeed, we left the ship in Derry very pleased with life. We had eaten high tea on board, we had breakfasted on board, we had spent the night in a real cabin and there had been just enough motion from the ship to let us admire our own hardihood. We hurried through the dingy streets of Derry—even yet no town in Britain has ever given me a more desperate appearance of grinding poverty—and made our way to a great-aunt's in Great James Street where we were talked into having a second breakfast. We noticed that the bacon was distinctly stronger-tasting than back home.

Our destination, Carndonagh, my father's village, was situated on the Inishowen Peninsula with Lough Foyle on one side of the neck of land and Lough Swilly on the other. It was less than ten miles from Malin Head, the most northerly point in the country, but by a truly Hibernian quirk it was for political purposes in the south, and it would be necessary for us to cross the border. Frank and I were eagerly looking forward to the border. We hoped from our experience of the films that we would be rigorously searched, certainly harshly spoken to, perhaps even maltreated.

There had been until 1931 a narrow-gauge railway line between Carndonagh and Derry but even thus early the motor car had proved triumphant and the Londonderry and Lough Swilly Railway Company had invested in buses, one of which we now boarded. The Customs officers proved disappointingly perfunctory and within an hour we were chugging up a decided hill into the Diamond, the hub of Carndonagh and the abode of my Irish grannie, my Uncle Willie and Aunt Mary, who were brother and sister to my father. The Diamond is a fairly common name for the market-place of small Irish towns, or more accurately perhaps, large Irish villages. From it ran the four streets of the settlement, Malin Street, Chapel Street, Bridge Street and Pound Street. The Diamond was the scene of the weekly market and the monthly fair and it was largely unpaved and at all times pungent.

My Uncle Willie was there to welcome us as we alighted stiffly from the bus. He was about 40, had a distinct resemblance to my father but was taller at nearly six feet and he had fair, greying hair, the decided, hooked, Crampsey nose which alone among the Crampsey males I lacked and piercing blue eyes. As we matched him in colouring we were soon identified as his kin wherever he took us. We found his quick Donegal accent hard to catch at first. Every other phrase seemed to be "God save us" or "Didja ever see an ould eedjit like yon?" He had a great aptitude for mimicry and exercised it on every possible occasion. He would run through his repertoire of local worthies and when we subsequently met these gentlemen it was often difficult to keep a polite gravity in one's expression.

My Aunt Mary also bore the family features; she tended to stoutness which, despite the fact that she never married, gave her an appearance of matronliness. She was the district nurse and in all weathers and at all hours pedalled her push-bike up the mountainous roads and tracks of Inishowen to confinements and cases of illness in those remote Donegal glens. Willie kept a pub, one of more than 30 licensed premises in a community of 900 souls and he also did some auctioneering and leasing of land. He was in addition the proprietor of the village football ground and therefore a man of some importance locally.

Frances, my grandmother, had been widowed a few months after

I was born. It would have been impossible to place her age more closely than between 60 and 75. She still had a very delicate complexion and I do not remember her wearing anything else but black. She spent much of her time in the upstairs sitting-room and did not often come down.

My father of course had no time to spend in Carn as all the natives called it and he returned to Glasgow the very next afternoon. Frank and I fought down a savage stinging of the eyes as his bus swung away down Chapel Street to the Derry Road and we were very severe on Philip who, despite his five years, was unmanly enough to be crying openly. Having given him to understand that he was disgracing himself and worse, us, we began to take stock of our new kingdom.

For a start, the family house in the Diamond would take some time to accept. There was no electric light, for that matter there was no gas light either, and we learned to read and play Ludo by the soft light of oil lamps. We went upstairs to bed for the first time in our lives and we climbed the staircase by candlelight. The lavatory was dry and at the bottom of the garden, a setting we had thought to be reserved exclusively for fairies. There were apple trees in the garden, gooseberry and blackcurrant bushes, and on one of the apple trees a swing had been slung. By dint of great effort you could work up on the swing until, over the roofs of Malin Street, you could see the sandhills of Lagg and beyond them the powerful, blue, open Atlantic. Altogether the garden was large, pleasant, functional and it lay beyond an earthen yard in which poultry scraped. In the yard there was a stack of turf, which in Scotland would have been called peat. It crumbled pleasantly between the fingers and burned much more aromatically if less efficiently than coal.

Everything around us was strange and new and on a bigger or more intensive scale somehow. Butter was saltier, bacon was stronger, the tea was like Hilaire Belloc's wine that tasted of the tar. My aunt was an especially good jam-maker and we made ferocious inroads on her apple jelly and gooseberry jam. Like almost everyone else in Carn she made her own bread—soda bread. I found this too heavy for my taste but even at that preferred it without the addition of caroway seed which seemed to be a local delicacy. By far the most popular dish with us boys was a Donegal standby known as "Poundies" in which potatoes were mashed up with leeks or syboes cut very fine and then some milk added. My father, even after all his years in Glasgow, and he had already been there for more than a score of years, retained his liking for country foods such as butter-milk and dulse but his sons' palates were too insipid for these.

We took some time to strike up any friendships with the Carn boys. We were fairly well endowed with cousins, real and putative, and on the day of my father's return to Glasgow we went down to the football field for a kickabout—just the three of us. We were of course objects of curiosity to the lads of the village and we were no sooner there than three or four of them drifted over and stood at the edge of the penalty area.

"Fire her out, then," said one, a lad in enormous boots and a blue frayed jersey whom we learned afterwards was a cousin, John Tully, and who became our closest friend. We had come down for a kick-about on our own but they were bigger and more numerous so, reluctantly, I "fired her out". In the bounce game that followed we were appalled by the savagery of the young Irish. They were crude hackers and would have been stigmatised as such in our native Glasgow district of Mount Florida.

We were to find that all games in Carn were played with incredible vigour for there is no harder breed of man on earth than the "mountainy men" of Donegal. Later that evening we went down to the field opposite the church where they were playing hurling, a game which resembles shinty in its skills, speed and ferocity. Even the girls played a variant of this, camogie, and a cousin of mine, Mary Grant, could run and climb with any of us. On Sunday afternoons there would be a football match between one of the Carn sides and a neighbouring village. Carn boasted three teams, Carndonagh Rangers, Carndonagh Celtic and the superbly named Carndonagh Doughnuts. One of the local curates played at wing-half for the Rangers and left no doubt at all by the vigour of his tackling that he regarded himself as one of the Church Militant. There was also a handball alley just along the street from our house where the locals hit a ball against the concrete wall with their fists in a manner reminiscent of the Basque pelota although at the time we were reminded of no such thing.

We had never lived in the country before and the agricultural aspects of life impressed us most strongly. The streets were full of animal deposits; once a week the Diamond echoed to a chorale of braying, neighing, cackling, bleating and squawking and it was then that for the only time in the week my uncle's shop lost its funereal aspect. There were small stalls with striped canvas awnings which sold combs, hair slides, patent medicines and beauty preparations.

The Cattle Show was Fair Day on a bigger scale with the extra ingredient of horse-jumping. For weeks beforehand, surrounding dykes, barns, and trees were placarded with advance notices of the show. We had a den in a hollow tree which lurched out over a little stream that fed the Glanagannon River. I never think of showjumping today without seeing that poster depicting a rider, immaculately accoutred and on a superb hunter, which for weeks I looked at as I plucked foxglove petals, flicked them into the incredibly clear water and tried to sink them with twigs. At the Cattle Show itself, the dress and standard of horseflesh was of a distinctly lower calibre.

In a variety of small ways we were made delightfully aware that we were in a foreign country. The pillar box into which we put our weekly letter home was of a different colour, the stamps had more variety than our unimaginative royal head. The coins had such exotic beasts as salmon and wolf-hounds on them and instead of our plodding, ponderous bobbies, there were the dark-faced, flat-hatted Gardai. From letters which came the other way we learned that my mother had stood up to the operation well and was on the mend.

With the letters came the sports papers which enabled us to keep pace with current events in Scottish football. These were delivered by the Carn postman, Gych, we never knew his real name though probability suggests he was a Doherty. He would poke his head round the shop door and shout "Mail! Glasgow Green!", a cry whose charm for us survived many repetitions. The newspapers were as important to us as the letters at that stage, indeed on one occasion we were vigorously reprimanded by my Aunt Mary for opening them first.

For entertainment we went twice a week to the Colgan Hall where they showed films. The audience sat on hard, wooden seats and to be well-fleshed was very helpful. I remember two of the films we saw there. One, appropriately enough, was *Parnell* with Clark Gable monumentally miscast as the Irish patriot. He was not well received by the locals, Parnell I mean. His work for Ireland counted little in the face of his attachment to Mrs O'Shea, for this last was the unforgivable sin in Donegal. My grannie conveyed this to me in a delicate way—he had run off with someone else's wife. Far better by north-west standards if he had been an alcoholic, a compulsive gambler or a wife-beater. Frances, my grandmother, "Ould Fannie" as Willie used in his more flippant moments to call her, had a great veneration for Gladstone and an engraving of the Grand Old Man shared pride of place with a sentimental reproduction of Pius XI.

The other film, which moved the audience to mass weeping, was *Captains Courageous* starring Spencer Tracy as a curly-headed Portuguese seaman and Freddy Bartholomew and Mickey Rooney as two young sprigs on a New England fishing boat on the Grand Banks. Poor Spencer died at sea but not before he had made a man of the distinctly cub-like Bartholomew. For weeks afterwards any attempt to sing his song, *Don't cry, Little Fishie*, was enough to set us off snivelling.

At the end of the performance in the Colgan Hall we would emerge to a darkness which we had not known to exist. The Glasgow of the 1930s was ablaze with neon signs and good street lighting, but in Carn on a starless night we found out what blackness meant. In view of what lay ahead it was an excellent preparation.

On fine days, and there were many, we stravaiged the surrounding country. We slid down the enormous sand-dunes at Lagg, scattering burnished grains as we came. On the superb, desolate beach at Ballyliffin the Crampseys could think of nothing more original to do than to play football. At the house of my cousin, Mary Grant, at Malin Head, we stood on the top of the cliffs, hundreds of feet above the water and watched the waves dash themselves against the first land of the Old World.

When the Donegal landscape was obscured by the gentle, drifting rain, or on, as the natives would have said a "gran' soft day" we stayed in and read. In the pub itself there was an elderly edition of *Pears Encyclopaedia* which I doggedly worked my way through. We all thought the famous advert featuring the tramp, "Dear Sir, many years ago I used your soap. Since then I have used no other...", was highly effective. There was also a book called *Pickwick in America* and through it I made my first contact with Dickens. There was a biography of Queen Christina of Sweden and an enormous history of Ireland. At the age of nine I was better acquainted with such characters in Irish history as O'Sullivan Beare and the White Knight of Kerry than at any time since.

We three boys must have been a sore torment to my childless aunt and uncle. We were constantly in bother, not so much from natural devilment as from a lack of understanding of country ways and country folk. Out for a walk one day we passed a blacksmith's forge and cottage. There was a pile of singed but unused turf which we began to throw industriously into the stream which flowed past the door. We were inclined to call streams those watercourses which the natives would have termed "sheughs" or ditches. The blacksmith came to the door of the forge, saw what we were doing and came at us with a bellow of righteous rage. "Gerra hell outa that, ye young buggers", and we gorra hell outa that. Unfortunately Frank, looking back to judge the closeness of the pursuit, ran full tilt into a barbed wire fence and left a considerable portion of his knee adhering to it.

He had an unfortunate run in that summer of 1939. When we stole wood from an old woman's hut, heaven knows why, it was Frank who collected a massive skelf or splinter in his finger, although I was the instigator of the raid. When we guddled farcically and ineffectively for trout, Frank would be the one to measure his length in the swift-flowing Glanagannon.

The predominant surname in that part of Inishowen was Doherty or O'Doherty. It was therefore necessary to distinguish individual clansmen by nicknames, since there might be as many as eight Patrick O'Dohertys living in a small compass. Hence one would be known as Paddy the Moss, another, walking with a stick, Paddy Three Legs, a third whose family had earlier flirted with emigration to the States, Paddy Oregon. The bynames were not always appreciated by the bearers of them and Phil once gave mortal though unwitting offence to a cross-eyed gentleman by addressing him with grave formality as "Mr Crookedshot", a title which his handicapped efforts at the dart board had gained for him.

We were irresponsible to a degree. About a mile out of Carn on the Malin Town road there is a bridge over an inlet of the Atlantic which is called the Trawbreaga Bridge. At high tide the water rushes in and the creek is deep and fast-flowing. The bridge has, or then had, a parapet about a foot wide. We were on this parapet, non-swimmers to a man, and I was teaching the others on very doubtful authority the steps of *The Lambeth Walk*, then enjoying a considerable vogue. So engrossed were we that we failed to notice the afternoon bus from Malin Head to Carn as it swept round the bend towards us. As it drew level the tyres squealed on the road, the driver threw out all anchors and a muffled "Jesus, Mary and Joseph" burst from the half-dozen or so passengers, among them my Aunt Mary. With great agility she was out of the bus, had scooped the three of us off the bridge and deposited us in the back seat of the vehicle. We got home to a well-merited hammering, my aunt asserting between blows that she had signed for three of us and was damned well going to return three of us.

That return was now, at the end of August, a matter of

immediacy. For some evenings, the battery radio in the stone-floored kitchen had been giving instructions (on the Northern Ireland region of the BBC) on the procedure to be followed in the event of war. Always the announcer would finish by saying, "War is not inevitable". Always Willie would add by way of epilogue, "Bloody liar". My mother had written to us twice a week and as I say had sent on our *Hotspurs, Adventures* and sports papers of a Saturday night but they intensified our longing and we were wearying for home.

The sensible thing to do, or at any rate the safe thing to do, would have been to stay where we were since in any war Eire would be neutral and Inishowen was about the most placid spot in Western Europe. We would not have it—we wanted back to Glasgow and my aunt was honest enough to admit that much as she had liked our company, she would be relieved to see us go. Early on the morning of Sunday, 3 September, my father arrived in Carn to collect us. He had crossed on a *Royal Ulsterman* crammed to the rails with evacuees and had come on by car from Belfast.

We sat in the kitchen and heard Neville Chamberlain make his broadcast. I remember the sense of his last few words rather than their exact form. "I have to tell you that no such reply has been received and, consequently, this country is now at war with Germany." As Chamberlain finished speaking, as his last phrase, "God save the King", died away, my father and uncle looked at each other, their minds inevitably moulded by their recollections of the First World War. Then, quietly, my father told us to get ready.

We left Carndonagh the following afternoon, having taken leave of our friends and foes. Willie came with us into Derry, possibly to make sure that we had no change of heart. On parting, my grandmother had given each of us a half-sovereign; she could hardly have expected to see us again nor in fact did she. Once again we crossed the border and this time the Northern Ireland guards were more thorough, doing their job with enjoyment and a consciousness of their own importance in an embattled community.

We went aboard an almost empty *Laird's Glen*, the signs of war already about her in her grey paint and blacked-out portholes. On the quayside a sparse crowd had gathered to see the equally sparse contingent sail. As we waited, another ship arrived from Glasgow, low in the water and with her decks crammed with people. Willie and my father again exchanged glances; clearly the latter wondered if he was doing the right thing in fetching us back.

On the quay an old fiddler was sawing away, playing melancholy tunes such as *Kathleen Mavourneen* and *The Bard of Armagh*, songs which will always be well received by those going into exile. Idly I reached into the pocket of my best brown suit and threw him a half-penny. To my amazement he stopped playing at once, called down on me the blessing of God, Patrick and Colmkille, and immediately made his way through the door of a dockside pub.

"What a to-do about a lousy halfpenny," I thought. "Lousy" was a very daring word and not to be spoken aloud; it was thus inevitably a constant in thought and *sotto voce* comment. As I thought it, a horrid suspicion struck me and I turned out my pockets. My fears were confirmed, my half-sovereign was in the palm of an old beggar. For him at least the war had started well.

The voyage back to Glasgow took 18 hours for we seldom proceeded above a crawl. Every piece of driftwood, every moving object was regarded as a potential U-boat. The telegraph clanged, the boat stopped. The skipper was entitled to be apprehensive for only the night before the *Athenia* had been sunk within a couple of hundred miles of where we were. Slowly we slipped down the River Foyle. On the Free State side the lights twinkled in the isolated houses, Robert Louis Stevenson's "Hollow valley, lamp-bestarred". On the Northern Ireland side there was impenetrable blackness. I should have looked at the Eire lights with more attention had I known that they would be the last that any of us would see for five years.

We turned in. The weather was mild and the cabin was sweltering since we could not open the portholes. Eventually we slept uneasily and when I awoke I was the first to shed blood for our country, forgetting about the hatch across the porthole and hitting my skull a stunning crack. By the time we had dressed and breakfasted we were off Gourock. Our old friends, the paddle steamers, were tied up at the pier forlornly, one or two already assuming wartime grey. For a brief moment in time we gazed at these beautiful craft, then we crawled up river. At Merklands Wharf we unloaded the cattle, always said to be more important than passengers to the Burns Laird Line, and almost at the same instant saw our first barrage balloon, like a tiny silver elephant in the cloudless sky.

My mother was there as we berthed and with her Julie, who had come on greatly since we left her. We bundled into a taxi, vaguely disappointed that there was no sign of air damage or indeed of any activity, and went off home through the drowsing, sunlit streets of the city at war.

Chapter Two

What time does the war start?

IN the sunny, lingering autumn of 1939, Mount Florida resembled nothing so much as Hamelin after the visitation of the Pied Piper. We had missed the mass evacuation which had denuded the Mount of schoolchildren, our friends were now scattered throughout the length and breadth of Scotland and my Aunt Julia, who was a primary teacher, had been evacuated with her charges to Bridge of Weir in Renfrewshire, only 15 miles from the centre of Glasgow but deemed to be a safe area.

For the first fortnight or so after the war broke out, the three Crampsey boys, fairish hair cut in fringes, stocky, blue-eyed and unruly, achieved a peak of popularity which was never attained again. It is clear now that the reason for this good reception was that our presence in the streets, whence all the rest had fled, was for the adults of Mount Florida a sign of normality. We made ourselves useful by going to the electrician's shop for the supplies of coloured electric light bulbs, candles and torches which were to be the stock in trade of forthcoming winters.

We watched, spellbound, as the one man in the street who had a private car fitted his two thicknesses of newspaper inside his side lights, leaving a small aperture for a beam of feeble light. We noticed that although the wardens who were charged with enforcing Air Raid Precautions were very vigilant in checking house lights—they would come through the closes into the back greens and yell gleefully and pompously, "Put out that light"—the black-out was at best partial since the glow from the great ironworks at Polmadie, "Dixon's Blazes", continued to light the sky for the better part of a year after the declaration of war. It was impossible, too, to do anything about the flashes that lit up the air where the tramcars crossed a set of points. It took some time to realise that the German bombers were not hovering aloft, poised to drop their load at the first chink from a scullery window.

There were few motor cars about after black-out time in those first weeks of the war and those that were had white-painted bumpers which gave them an eerie appearance. As was bound to happen, many civilians took instructions all too trustingly and literally. I remember seeing an old neighbour of ours with the tears coursing down her cheeks as she returned from the Cat and Dog Home. She had just had her small terrier put down, as there was no gas-mask provision for animals and the poor soul lived in hourly expectation of air raids in which gas would be used.

My brothers and I were not ordained to live very long in our splendid isolation as gradually the evacuees crept back to the city from the fastnesses of Inveraray, Lundin Links and Lamlash, queering our pitch. My great friend, Bill, had been evacuated with his twin sister to the village of Kirkmichael in Ayrshire where the only event of the day was the arrival of the bus from Maybole. When, six weeks after the outbreak of war, the Luftwaffe had failed to put in an appearance, his constant demands for repatriation were met. We were delighted to see him, as his absence had resulted in all kinds of temporary but basically unsatisfactory alliances.

For almost the first year of the war there was no great upheaval in the lives we led. At 39 my father would not be called up except in the direst of emergencies; he used to refer to himself as "Britain's last hope". Ration books had been issued almost from the start of hostilities but the quantities allocated were ample and only the most basic foods were in any way restricted. The absence of light was the great difference as October drew into November. Each of us was issued with a torch for our excursions to the café for cigarettes and ice-cream and our natural agility, to say nothing of our fear of the dark, meant that we covered the length of Clincart Road in not much more than 30 seconds.

The uneventful nature of those first months was something of a real disappointment and we felt vaguely let down by the Germans. What was the point of a war when nothing was happening? There were signs that we were at war, our windows were criss-crossed with paper strips as a protection against blast and black-out material for curtains was bought in hundreds of thousands of yards. We carried our gas-masks everywhere and our young sister, Julie, had a Mickey Mouse model which was somehow far more horrific than the orthodox kind, but not much was happening. Cinemas and football grounds were shut and we seemed much more likely to die of boredom rather than at the hands of the enemy.

The weather was marvellously warm and we played in the streets, singing the songs of the time, *Run Rabbit Run* and *The Siegfried Line*. One of the boys, Graham Clinging, a blameless youth but no footballer and therefore not greatly esteemed by us, won a certain local acclaim by pretending to give war-time broadcasts. His opening announcement

> Calling all cars, calling all stations,
> Hitler's lost his combinations

sent some but not all of us into kinks of laughter. As the war progressed he added the infamous Lord Haw-Haw to his repertoire. It might have been thought that Lord Haw-Haw's broadcasts from Germany were well enough known not to need Graham's endorsement. They were the very stuff of rumour and everybody could recount how on the previous evening William Joyce (to use his real name) had stated positively that the town clock at Reading or Godalming or Tunbridge Wells or wherever had stopped at ten to three after the air-raid of the night before.

Servicemen took a surprisingly long time to appear. The first I remember were the airmen who formed the crew of the barrage-balloon which was moored on a site next to the duck-pond in the Queen's Park. At first large crowds came to gawk as the airmen self-consciously and importantly inflated their monstrous captive but gradually interest dwindled as the performance became routine. By about November soldiers began to appear on the streets in quantity. Mount Florida School had been commandeered and would remain in the hands of the military for almost the whole of the war. The troops paraded in Queen's Park Recreation Ground and the streets of the Mount rang with the tramp of burnished boots as a platoon or company of conscripts marched awkwardly down Prospecthill Road in new, coarse, ill-fitting uniforms. As they drilled, some of the older Mount boys used to jeer at them, "Fourteen shillings a week", that being the entitlement of a private soldier at the time. I found the crassness of the remark jarring then and I still do.

Early in the war my father brought home an ornate war map of Europe, published by one of the newspapers. It purported to carry an assessment of the military, naval and air power of every European state and contained such items as "Rumania has 500 first-line aircraft and 1200 second-line ones". This was of course sheer legend—if there were 1700 Rumanians in the air in 1939 then a considerable proportion of them were on brooms—but we believed it implicitly and thought what a help the Rumanians would be if they threw in their lot with the Allies. With the map also came little flags to mark the changing position of the front line. I was keen on this at first but the inertia of the winter soured me, for with the exception of a spasm in which the Allies took Saarbrucken, absolutely nothing happened on the Western Front before Christmas.

In the matter of schooling I was extremely fortunate. Mount Florida School, as I have said, was lost to the Glasgow Corporation Education Department for years and many of my friends were on half-time instruction as late as 1942. The school which I attended, Holy Cross, was older and smaller and was therefore not required. As early as October 1939 we were doing a couple of hours a day. As yet there were very few children back in the city, at least in our district, and we met quite often in the informal atmosphere of the staff-room. We did little by way of set lessons but we had reassumed the habit of school and that in itself was important.

We enjoyed being taught in a coal-fired room by a pretty young teacher, Miss Kerr. She had been in Finland in the summer of 1938 and when the Russians invaded that country just before Christmas 1939, she told us of her holiday there. All I remember is that she thought that the Finns were a most honest people. For years afterwards I knew that if one was going to mislay an umbrella, then Helsinki was the place in which to do it for a gaggle of honest Finns in relentless pursuit would undoubtedly restore it. On another occasion, a young male teacher, awaiting his call-up and understandably not too involved in things educational, told us graphically what he was going to do to the Germans when he joined the Royal Air Force. Alas, varicose veins meant that he had to sublimate his aggression in the National Fire Service!

Apart from the absence of the marvellous glittering lights, the first Christmas of the war was perfectly normal. There was an abundance of food, sweets and toys and the call-up had made practically no inroad on the young men of the district. It was in truth a low-key war, there was not the market for the rush of volunteers who had answered the call back in 1914. In the increasingly sophisticated warfare of the 1930s the untrained man was more of a nuisance than anything else, no matter how genuine his enthusiasm.

The first action of the war which had given us legitimate cause for pride was the Battle of the River Plate which led to the scuttling of the German pocket battleship *Graf Spee*. We played out this dramatic episode in the streets. Curiously there was great competition to be a German officer, in particular the ill-fated Captain Langsdorf who had commanded the vessel and gone down with it. This part was usually annexed by Philip, whose rendition of it consisted of strutting around with arm extended in Nazi salute and barking at everyone within earshot, "Very good, Herr Kapitan Deutschland". It had to be the worst impersonation going but it was difficult to convince a five-year-old of this.

We were of course the first generation that could see the events of the war on screen with great rapidity and this we were able to do when the cinemas reopened as they soon did in response to public clamour. I conceived an overwhelming dislike for the voice or rather the voices employed by the newsreel commentators. They had three well-defined manners of delivery, the Mark One, Britain Can Take It, the Mark Two, Britain Can Dish It Out and the Mark Three, Heavily Facetious. All three were hectoring and the most extreme form of Mark Three came after the entry of Italy into the war and the capture of an Italian Division in the desert by Wavell's troops. There was a long-distance shot of men trudging across the sands to the prison cages while the commentator, never beyond Wardour Street, trolled, "They look pretty dejected but they'll feel better after a meal and a shower—that is if you can ever clean a Wop." So intensely angry did this kind of nonsense make me that I used to react by cheering whenever Hitler or Mussolini appeared on screen, thereby attracting annoyed glances from other cinema-goers and furious embarrassed punches from my brothers who had no wish to be tarred with my momentarily unpatriotic brush.

In the early weeks we were often at the cinema, for football took some time to get back on the rails and when it did a gas-mask had to be presented along with the price of admission. The Scottish League had been scrapped for the duration of the war and Eastern and Western Regional Leagues substituted. This meant that attractive visitors such as Aberdeen, Dundee, Hearts and Hibernian were seen no more and it seemed to us that Dumbarton and Airdrieonians were poor replacements. In feeling this we were very irrational and ungrateful since our beloved Queen's Park had actually been relegated to the Second Division in 1939 and but for the intervention of Hitler, Dumbarton and Airdrieonians would have been our staple diet. For the first few months of the war there was a crowd limit of 15,000 at Hampden as it was felt that the great stadium would offer a ready-made target from the air. My mother approved of this restriction since we lived a mere 400 yards from the ground but in view of the apathetic conduct of the war the crowd limit was soon raised.

The coming of war converted the radio from a toy to a national utility. Increasingly, people would stop whatever they were doing, work or play, to listen to the six o'clock and the nine o'clock news. It was curiously similar to the way that farm labourers during the summer in Donegal had broken off for the Angelus bell. Within a year of war the announcers had lost their anonymity and became immediately identifiable, members of the family almost.

There was a crop of war songs, distressingly banal and in the strict sense vulgar. *Roll Out the Barrel* and *We're Going to Hang Out the Washing on the Siegfried Line* were played incessantly, imposing their spurious Cockney geniality (for all that the first-named song was German-American) on the scene. A patriotic lad was bound to believe that our Army, Navy and Air Force were unsurpassed but it did seem unlikely that German song-writers were inferior.

Nor could I share the general liking for *Garrison Theatre* which brought Jack Warner to prominence. It seemed to be like so many subsequent British radio shows, a collection of catch phrases tied together with string. "Blue pencil", "Mind my Bike" and "Rill mill" became part of our mindless conversational currency. Our wireless set at the time was a battery one and provided the batteries were kept charged it gave good reception, free of mains hum. My special care was the accumulators and once a week I took them to Munn's the electrical shop to have them charged. This was a message that I never minded going for; apart from anything else, Mr Munn always gave me a new, sharpened pencil, but disaster struck on one occasion when I slipped in the snow and the acid from the accumulators burned a hole in my brand-new navy trenchcoat. I resented the hammering I got all the more because for once I had been totally·guiltless.

The radio service in the first instance abolished regional programmes and later on went on to Home and Forces networks. There seemed to be nothing on the radio in the very earliest days of war except news bulletins and Sandy Macpherson at the theatre organ who played interminably on an instrument on which it is not possible to make a noble sound. Gone for the time were the great pre-war dance bands which I had listened to spellbound, those of

Lew Stone, Harry Roy, Carroll Gibbons, Nat Gonella and Roy Fox. I had been greatly excited when my Scots grandmother, who lived in Kinning Park, told me that a girl who lived near her, Mary Lee, had gone off to London to become a singer, or crooner as we invariably called them, with Roy Fox's band. This seemed the height of success and sophistication. Most famous of all, even more famous than Ambrose, was Henry Hall whose "Good evening, this *is* Henry Hall speaking", I then thought the height of affectation, although "putting it on" would more probably have been the phrase I muttered sourly to myself.

So, in a warm, well-lit house with the coloured globes on the Christmas tree and the paper stars and bells which made up "the decorations", the first Christmas of the war came and went. We listened to the King's Christmas broadcast and made arrangements to see the Queen's Park-Third Lanark game on New Year's Day. The adults agreed that neither side was interested in the slightest in actually fighting this war and that peace would come soon.

Chapter Three

The start

FOR us three boys 1940 made a bad beginning. At the last moment our mother decided that we should go with her to my Grannie McNaughton's house in the early afternoon of New Year's Day, thereby passing up the Queen's Park versus Third Lanark Ne'erday match. It was decided, and not even optimistic appeals to my father, normally a receptive audience, could overturn the decree. We therefore set off by tramcar to my grandmother's house in Kinning Park through a city oddly bare of men. They were either at football matches or had failed to put in an appearance from the night before after their strenuous Hogmanay exertions.

We were in sullen mood as we climbed the stairs to my grandmother's small tenement house flat in Cowie Street. We were well-enough dressed as was our New Year custom. Suits were seldom new by January but such things as gloves, scarves and caps were, having arrived from aunts and courtesy aunts with the Christmas mail. Our sulkiness grew with the realisation that the adult male members of the family and friends were at a football match all right, the Rangers-Celtic game, then as now a compulsive tribal ritual for much of the city. My real and courtesy uncles were firm Celtic supporters, though by no means virulent ones, and they returned depressed or elated according to how the day had gone. Their loyalty to Parkhead aroused that dour streak in me which was always a light sleeper and for a couple of years, out of pure cussedness, I gave my heart to Rangers before transferring my affiliations permanently to the local side, Queen's Park.

I loved my grandmother's house, although in truth it had little to commend it. It was on the first floor of a dilapidated tenement and was one of three doors on an inky-black, wooden-floored landing. During the hours of darkness outside, and even during daylight, for it was invariably mirky inside the close, the landing was lit by a hissing gas-mantle in a square glass which intensified rather than softened the gloom of the stairway.

Two things since the start of the war had made these closes even more Stygian than before. The closemouth light was dimmed and across the front of the close was constructed a baffle wall, made of sandbags and corrugated iron, the construction of which it was hoped would drastically reduce the effects of blast from bomb explosions. These baffle walls passed at once into Glasgow myth and legend as tales were recounted of thousands of families who, buying their furniture on the never-never, now happily stopped payment in the joyous knowledge that there was not enough room between baffle wall and close entrance for the furniture to be taken out by repossessors.

For all its defects I thought my grandmother's house a fascinating one. It had an inside toilet but no bathroom and the kitchen had the one tap, gleaming, brass, cold water. All the water had to be heated in the big iron kettle that sang gently on the glittering steel range. This last was my granny's treasure even when it had to be black-leaded and I can yet see the yellow tins of Zebo with their screw caps, which I then thought had something to do with the Zoo. At the back, the kitchen window looked on to a busier railway line than ours in Mount Florida and in front the room window looked across Scotland Street directly into McNeill's Forge, whence there was always the hum of heavy machinery.

We had been forbidden the match because we had to be fed and watered first—no other logistical system would work in that tiny house. The menu could scarcely have been more traditional: home-made broth, roast beef with roasted potatoes, mashed potatoes and Brussels sprouts, and trifle. Later we found that this was called Scotch trifle but it never occurred to us that there was any other kind. The house was just round the corner from the Creamola works in Lambhill Street and almost every Glasgow child learned the word "Creamola" before he learned the word "custard". We loved the slogan "Tickles the world's palate" and our admiration was not at all diminished in that we thought it was "Tickles the world's plate". In like manner we found the Camp Coffee poster very affecting with its officer and loyal Indian bearer above the stern advice "Don't be misled", although we had no very clear idea of how one was mizzled.

I loved to stay in my grandmother's house and frequently did since my brothers had an agreeable habit of catching such things as

30

whooping cough, measles and chickenpox at different times from myself and always first, so that I was sent down to Kinning Park for isolation. In the warm atmosphere of the house on New Year's Day 1940 we bit by bit recovered our good humour and behaved tolerably well during the songs that the adults insisted on singing afterwards. My father had a pleasant though very light tenor voice and his great song was *Moira, my girl*. Uncle Tommy, not a real uncle, needed little encouraging to sing *Nirvana*. He was a tall, thin, almost cadaverous man who had an oddly powerful bass voice. We thought *Nirvana* was a terrible song, all about dumb gods being shattered. My grandmother, who had a wavery soprano, rarely failed to sing *Dark Lochnagar*. She would always pause on the penultimate word in the line before making her assault on the last note,

England thy beauties are tame . . . and . . . domestic
For one who has roamed on the mountains afar,
O for the crags that are wild . . . and . . . majestic
The steep frowning glories of dark Lochnagar.

We did not always retain the degree of composure that good manners would have dictated. We ourselves had to recite or play the piano. My staple diet at that time was *Hemy's Piano Tutor* and I remember entertaining the company that New Year with the Japanese Imperial National Anthem. It had no significance whatsoever, there was no war to speak of and if someone had turned on the street lights outside it would have been the only major difference that we would have noticed over the last three months.

I have referred to my grandmother's house but in fact my grandfather, Robert McNaughton, after whom I was named, did not die until a few days later, before the decorations were taken down on Twelfth Night. He had been a blacksmith as a young man but suffered terribly from arthritis and had been totally crippled since the age of 34. His hands were twisted beyond recognition and he could not grip anything at all. His pain was constant and he moaned pitiably as he was turned in bed, although he never failed to put a face on things for visitors. My Aunt Julia who was young and pretty lived at home with her parents and Bob McNaughton liked nothing better than when some of her friends came round to play cribbage, whist or just to chat.

Now, on the fourth of January, he was dead. I was not of an age to feel great sorrow for a death but I could and did feel a great guilt. This was because a few years before I had told my mother, falsely,

31

that my grandfather had died. I made out that my Aunt Julia had told me in school (she taught there) and the story was fiendishly plausible. My mother could and did clout us on need but on this occasion her gentle "Why did you say that, son?" was infinitely more effective than slaps, flytings or reproaches. I do not know whether I did it for dramatic effect or as a joke in execrable taste. I do know that as a boy I never did a worse action.

We buried my grandfather on a frosty day, not in either of the two traditional Catholic cemeteries but in a newly opened one in Barrhead. His was one of the first dozen interments. For my brothers, free of my particular shame, it was a day when one rode in a big car and had a day off school, acquiring a certain importance in the playground next day.

My grandmother was very distressed. Her married life had been hard, she had never been free of money worries and in recent years the nursing of her husband had become increasingly onerous. She had hardly ever had a holiday since her marriage and even to spend a night away from home was the rarest of events. Yet she had gone about the little house in Cowie Street singing, in the words of her husband, "like a lintie". The house resounded to the notes of *After the Ball Was Over*, *Ma Donna Clara* and other songs of her girlhood. With the death of my grandfather her life would be infinitely easier but she was almost beyond consolation. To add to her worries she could see that my mother suffered from the same complaint as her father and that the long-term prospects were distinctly bad.

The funeral was a watershed in one sense. It was the very last time that all the young men who had been in the habit of coming around the house were at a gathering together. One of them had already received his calling-up papers, another was going to England on war work.

The winter bit late and bit savagely. It snowed for almost five weeks and when the thaw came it came too quickly, with burst pipes making life a damp, oozing mess. Water in Mount Florida was cut off for days at a time and we carried water in buckets from stand-pipes for the neighbours. We were strictly forbidden to accept any money for doing this but the three of us agreed that it would be impolite to refuse stubbornly where there seemed to be a genuine wish to recognise our services.

Weather came like a thief in the night because now there were no weather forecasts. Sometimes the effects were ludicrous. On that very same New Year's Day on which we had been cruelly deprived of seeing Queen's Park entertain Third Lanark, the traditional Edinburgh Derby match had been played between Hibernian and Heart of Midlothian at Easter Road. This was a bizarre encounter to say the least, as visibility in the capital on that day was less than ten yards. Nevertheless, since the cancellation of the game might have given valuable intelligence to the Luftwaffe, although what they could have done with ten yards visibility is unclear, the game had to go ahead. The spectators saw nothing, most of the players saw very little and the Hearts winger, Donaldson, was actually stranded on the field for some considerable time after the final whistle, unaware that the game had come to an end.

The snow and ice stayed with us through January and much of February causing great hardship but conferring one unexpected benefit, because the lying snow made it rather easier to see at night. Food rationing was introduced just after New Year but at first only butter, ham, bacon and sugar were restricted in quantity. I had gone back to a half-day at school on a regular basis and indeed before very long was in attendance all day. I was also looking for a job.

I needed a job, coming up to ten years of age, because I needed a bike. I was mortified at still having to make my excursions on the trike which I had had since my fifth birthday. It was a very large, tank-like vehicle but all my friends had long since graduated to fairy cycles as the 16-inch wheel variety were called. I had taken the trike on considerable and far-ranging expeditions, to Clarkston and Carmunnock, but as a means of propulsion it was becoming grotesque and I should have to do something about it. I had already decided to miss out the intermediate stage of the fairy cycle and go straight to the 18-inch variety.

I felt that I had a lot to offer employers, not least my previous work experience. In the summer of 1938 and again for a glorious fortnight in 1939 I had been the right-hand lad of the local milkman, Louis Muirhead. Louis had blond wavy hair, a horse and cart and a way with the housewives. It was my fondest dream to sit up with him in his cart behind the black horse which pulled it, and be allowed to go back with it to the stables next to the Kingsway cinema.

I got my wish under stressful circumstances. In the summer of 1938 the corduroy jerkins which were called lumber-jackets were all the rage with Mount Florida boys. They were fairly expensive and I had not worn mine for above a week before I lost it. I had put it down to use as a goalpost in the Recreation Ground and come away without it. When I retraced my steps in search of it, it was not to be found. On reporting home my mother created what seemed to be a totally disproportionate fuss. I was told to get back to the Recreation Ground at once and to "Get the jerkin—and if you don't you needn't come back". I failed to find the damned jerkin and was moodily making my way home when I was hailed by the passing Louis. He knew that I had long wanted to come out with him and one of his usual delivery boys had failed to show up. There was no need to ask me twice. I swung myself up, put my feet on the driving board and away we went.

By any objective standard, Louis Muirhead was an extremely handsome young man and in a spotless white, open-necked shirt and well-cut jodhpurs he must have had a powerful effect on the young housewives of King's Park. He would leap the low hedges with a crate of milk slung over each arm and the welcome he got at the doors indicated that the ladies of the district appreciated their luck in having the milk delivered by a matinee idol. I was oblivious of time on that first morning with him and on my return late that afternoon I was met three streets from home by frantic outrunners dispatched by my mother who feared that I had taken her parting strictures all too literally. The sober truth was that by that time I had forgotten all about the wretched jerkin and my mother was at such a pitch of anxiety that she would not have minded if I had lost every stitch that I stood up in. I continued to go on the milk cart for several weeks and got sixpence a day for my services, a gross overpayment. With the money, I put red savings-stamps in a Post Office Savings Book and the bike began to seem a possibility when the summer in Ireland put paid to the milk round, since Louis had clearly to find another right-hand lad.

The early weeks of the war had provided a temporary windfall which was lucrative while it lasted. There was a searchlight battery stationed near the Old Snuffmill Bridge in Cathcart and I had come across them while out on the trike one day. I started talking to a bored sentry and he mentioned that the local shop had failed to deliver their daily order of lemonade and soft drinks. I offered to fill the gap and was allowed to take back the empties and keep the refund money on them. For three glorious weeks or so I was the self-appointed Gunga Din to the unit and then one morning on reporting for duty I found the field empty and the tents folded and gone. Something more permanent was needed.

In the late spring of 1940 I persuaded a local newsagent to let me deliver evening papers and as the Germans invaded Norway and

Denmark, then Holland, Belgium and France, the inhabitants of Florida Avenue, Florida Square and Florida Crescent got the latest news from me. Suddenly the war had caught alight at the very time when people were talking about a decided return to peace-time conditions. There had been moves for a relaxation of the black-out regulations, the Scottish Football League was actively canvassing for a return to the pre-war set-up in football, and there were demands for a better steamer service to the Clyde coast resorts.

All of that went in those few hectic weeks in April and May of 1940. We rushed quickly to the war map to see how many planes the Norwegians had. The Danes were already out of things, much to our disgust. The news was not reassuring. The Norwegians had very few planes, unlike the Rumanians, and most of those that they had were seaplanes. Yet they were making a fight of it and it looked as if we had recorded a genuine victory at Narvik. Then, for the first time in the war the tell-tale phrases began to appear—"objectives attained", "retired to prepared positions". In a few weeks we had the most tangible evidence of defeat in the presence in Mount Florida School of the *Chasseurs Alpins*, the "Alpine Shassoors" in local received pronunciation. They were not the first foreign troops to be seen in the district as there were already a few Poles and would shortly be many more. My Aunt Julia had befriended a Polish airman, Frantisek, and he was a frequent visitor to my grandmother's house. My aunt learned to play, and we learned to sing, the English translation of the Polish National Anthem.

> Poland's soul has not departed while we live to own her,
> What by might was taken from us might will yet recover,
> March, march, Dombrowski, fight for liberation,
> With your arm to lead us, we will free the nation.

We particularly liked the "March, march, Dombrowski" bit and felt very fierce and martial as we sang it. We noticed also that the Poles were better uniformed and smarter than our own troops and wondered why this should be so. Our chief interest at the moment remained the Alpine Shassoors and we went down to look at them — talking to them was out of the question — every night. One of our number claimed to be able to talk to them and earned great kudos from the casual way he delivered the phrase "Ally zongferr, restiley skwee" which he maintained meant "Go to hell and stay there". For my part I could not compete with such a sophisticate.

Norway went and I continued to deliver newspapers. The elders of the family and the neighbours were unanimous that there was much to hope for from the Belgians; they had shown Fritz what was what in the Kaiser's war. Leopold, the king, would be as stubborn as his father Albert the Good had been and the Belgian troops were excellent. The almost immediate surrender of Belgium came therefore like a thunderclap. A generation conditioned to the agonisingly slow progress of the Great War could not come to terms with the appalling speed of events. After all, the war in Spain had taken three years to resolve.

Still, events in the Low Countries were seen as a temporary setback. The French *poilu* knew his onions, as a thousand and three comedians said, and would sort out the Boche. The Maginot Line was certain to stop the Germans, it was so good that it had underground railways and cinemas, a far cry from the lousy, sodden trenches of 25 years before. I continued to deliver the papers and read the sports pages with great interest, for Scotland were going to play England at Hampden Park in the first really big match since the outbreak of war. It would not be quite the glorious occasion of peace-time. Mount Florida boys were the ultimate in connoisseurs of the big match but we were not disposed to be too sniffy, even although the attendance was restricted to 75,000, just half of the number that had swarmed through the streets to the great games of the late 1930s.

To be a boy living in Mount Florida conferred a unique, unearned distinction. Literally round the corner from him was the famous Hampden Park, then and for long after the largest football stadium in the world. On an international or Cup Final day the Mount was a thrilling place as relays of trams, buses and trains released their quotas of football followers from all over Scotland and far beyond. Our favourite vantage point for such occasions before the war was The Well. This was a lugubrious, cast-iron structure, dedicated to Queen Victoria in a vague way and it stood at the junction of Cathcart Road and Clincart Road. Here on matchdays everyone alighted and we would have been at our stance since ten o'clock in the morning, pestering men for the silver paper from their cigarette packets, or, better still, for cigarette cards. The actual matches had then been forbidden to us, a wise precaution, for those were the days of attendance records and a ground with more than 149,000 people in it was not the place for a seven-year-old boy. Now, in 1940, the first wartime hardships had begun to bite, cigarette cards were on the way out and those English supporters who witnessed the 1-1 draw were very much for the most part in uniform.

There was going to be no drawn match on the Continent, that was becoming increasingly clear to the few who had the perception to see. To most people, however, the collapse of France came like a lightning bolt. That the Germans would occupy large tracts of France was almost taken for granted. It had happened in 1914, but that the French would throw in their hand was never contemplated. I had gone to the cinema with a complimentary ticket from my newsagent's shop—one of the great perks of the job. The cinema was the Govanhill and the film *Gulliver's Travels*. I came out into the sunny May evening humming a song from the film, *Come home again, you sailor man*, when I became aware of newsboys selling a special edition. Paris had fallen and when I told my mother this on my return home she wept for the only time in the war that I can remember. I did not know that she was five months pregnant and that, surer with every year that she had inherited her father's arthritis, she had reason enough to weep.

The French withdrew from the war and the "Alpine Shassoors" marched away with dazed faces and, at long intervals, tear-stained faces. A new name was added to the category of those who had to be hissed whenever they appeared on newsreels at the cinema, Marshal Pétain who had taken over the leadership of the demoralised French. He had been a hero of the First World War and had drawn the obvious conclusion from the war memorials of the smallest French villages but we belonged to a hard school and could not forgive him withdrawing France from the fight. The country held its breath when it seemed that the whole of the British Expeditionary Force must be trapped in Northern France and released it when the troops got way from Dunkirk. We were thankful for deliverance and the newspapers made much of it but nobody basically believed that it was all part of a grand strategic plan.

We were on our own and, to tip the scales further, we now had to contend with Italy. The circumstances of the Italian entry at a time when the French were down and out made the news peculiarly unpalatable and fury found its expression in the stoning and looting of a great many Italian cafés and restaurants in Glasgow. I cannot recall this happening in Mount Florida although it may well have done, but the local Kinning Park café, Benny's, across the street from my grandmother, was certainly put to the sack, and for weeks afterwards carried across its boarded windows, "The proprietor is a

British subject", a piece of information which had come too late to do any good. It is doubtful if it would have served in any event as the Italian declaration of war allowed many youths who had not been to the fore in the rush of volunteers to work off their xenophobic prejudices. In certain districts these were the more acceptable because anti-Catholic.

Our revenge on the Italians took a more subtle form in that they were simply not taken seriously as combatants. It so happened that the first British success of any scale on land was against the Italians in Libya and Somaliland. The result was the firm conviction among our civilian population that the Italians simply could not fight. The *Beano*, always in the forefront of wartime humour, brought out a comic strip entitled Musso da Wop ("He's a big a da flop"). Riddles abounded, such as "Why does Musso never change his socks? Because he smells defeat." The *Beano*, which had no great opinion of the intelligence of its readers, made things easy for them by putting "de feet" in brackets. To make jokes about Hitler was more difficult because the man was basically much more frightening.

Now it seemed very probable that we would be invaded. Road blocks began to appear even on the most innocent of country roads, cylindrical blocks of concrete which allowed only one vehicle to pass at a time. The road blocks were manned by those volunteers who for a few days were called parashots, then Local Defence Volunteers and finally the Home Guard. In this direst of emergencies it is odd to record that the services of the Home Guard were not received with universal approval. The Mount Florida platoon had commandeered the smaller of the Hampden pitches, Lesser Hampden, and taken over the pavilion as their headquarters only to suffer the indignity of being evicted by the Hampden groundsman, Jimmy Ritchie. A *modus vivendi* was eventually arrived at and the Home Guard did a valuable job in assisting with fire-watching at the great stadium.

We kept a wary eye out for paratroops and stretches of level ground such as golf course fairways were covered with rows of poles to make landing by enemy aircraft impracticable. We knew from our papers and spy stories that paratroopers would probably come dressed as nuns as apparently the Low Countries had been infested by Nazis in this disguise during the brief campaign there. Cars were to be put out of action at night but it was thought wise to caution against an excess of zeal and remind the population that in their midst there were many foreign allied soldiers whose lack of command of English in no way betokened enemy sympathies.

As though the world were completely normal, my mother took her family to Kirn for the summer. The only concession to the emergency was that we had a fortnight instead of the usual month, something which we considered a great let-down. Kirn was as bustling as it had been in peace-time summers, perhaps more so, but already it was decidedly more drab and there was an absence of colour.

Holidays before the war had been marvellous and of course not everything was changed. There were still a few brightly panelled beachballs in the ironmongers and the last of the Mickey Mouse pails. The lending library on a quick check retained the copies of *The Fifth Form at St Dominic's* and *Rob Wylie's Luck* which were going to do us on wet days throughout our reduced stay. The pier was there, twin-towered, onion-domed and privately owned as befitted the status of Kirn which was regarded by its visitors as distinctly a cut above Dunoon. Hunter's Quay, the next pier along, thought of itself as even more upmarket since its Marine Hotel was the centre of action for much of the Clyde yachting fortnight.

It was on the water that we noticed the difference. The big yachts had gone and would not be back. The private steam yachts, so much a feature of the 1930s, had been commandeered for Dunkirk or laid up. Above all, the steamer service had been cut back to the bone. We could and did in previous years spend entire days on the coal pier at Kirn watching the comings and goings of the river steamers, resplendent in their various liveries. There were the yellow funnels and black hulls of the LMS boats with aristocratic names, such as the *Duchess of Fife*, the *Marchioness of Lorne* and the *Marchioness of Breadalbane*. There were the white funnel boats which we loved because they came all the way from Glasgow, the *Queen Empress*, the *Eagle III* and the *Kylemore*, with the turbines *King Edward* and *Queen Mary II*. All the LNER boats from Craigendoran, most colourful with grey hulls and red, white and black funnels, were called after the characters of Sir Walter Scott, hence *Kenilworth*, *Marmion, Lucy Ashton, Talisman, Jeannie Deans, Waverley*. The MacBrayne ship, first of all the *Columba* and latterly the *Saint Columba*, did not condescend to call at Kirn and we had to be content with a glimpse from afar as she made the diagonal crossing from Gourock to Dunoon, bearing her complement of English to the shooting lodges of West Argyllshire.

To have been a boy in the last five years before the war and to have seen the surpassingly beautiful Clyde paddlers was to have seen the Old South in the week before they fired on Fort Sumter. Our long holidays had been strictly regulated by the arrival and departure of the steamers with their elegantly raked funnels, slim, tapering masts and marvellously intricate scroll-work on the fanned paddle-boxes.

We lived in a flat in a row of tall tenements known as Argyll Terrace and from it I used to run down the stony lane at the back of Kirn Brae in the heat-hazy morning. Across the river the Cloch Lighthouse lowed mournfully but unconcernedly; you could almost hear it say, "This will lift by ten". Shirt, shorts and sandals constituted my complete rig but I never felt cold as I sped down to Ross's Dairy for the rolls. If I were to time, the white-funneled *Kylemore* was in at the pier on her way up-river from Rothesay to Glasgow. She returned at four in the afternoon and that was the signal for us to leave the paddling-pond where we were lying flat-out, pushing ourselves along with our hands firmly on the bottom, under the impression that we were swimming.

If I were a few minutes late in the morning, the *Kylemore* had gone and the *Caledonia* had tied up. She was a commuter as opposed to a cruise ship and she served Kilmun, Strone, Blairmore and the other hamlets of the Holy Loch and Loch Long. She too was a paddler but we had not the same affection for her, purely because her paddle-boxes were concealed and from broadside on it was very difficult to tell that she was not actually a turbine steamer. I suppose that the effect was that of a very cunningly cut maternity dress, although of course I did not so rationalise it at the time. I was outraged because the *Caledonia* seemed to be ashamed of being a paddler and all my love was given to those ships that were paddlers, naked and unashamed.

I was never drawn to the turbine steamers in anything like the same degree. In some undefined way I felt that their increasing numbers on the Clyde threatened my well-established boyish world and, looking back, I believe that I was right so to think. I admired the beauty of miniature liners such as the *Duchess of Montrose* and the *Duchess of Hamilton*. The *Queen Mary II* was interesting as having been actually the original *Queen Mary*, the numeral having been added to accommodate Cunard when the great liner was given that name. Perhaps unexpectedly, Williamson-Buchanan, who owned the river steamer felt no sense of honour in giving way but rather one of grievance that their name had been appropriated. We were proud too of the *King Edward*, the world's first passenger-carrying turbine steamer, but it had no secure corner in our hearts. That was reserved for the paddle-steamers.

Now, with the war, the paddlers had largely gone. They were a better bet for mine-sweeping than the turbine steamers. Many of the latter remained on the upper Firth but had been taken out of passenger service and remained at Gourock to ferry ashore the troops who were already arriving from Canada and who would later come from Australia, New Zealand and the United States. We could no longer spend the day sitting on the coal-jetty next to Kirn pier and watching the big paddles or the screws churn the green, translucent water to a white, foaming ginger-beer. The 30 steamers of 1939 were reduced to three, grubby in their grey warpaint, and the sturdy cargo boats, the *Arran*, the *Minard* or the *Ardyne* which came in and unloaded crates and cartons for the grocers, bags of fertilisers for the farmers, and, occasional and rare delight, a flitting. These plodding little boats were going on to call at villages all the way down to Campbeltown and offered a puritanical reminder that the world was still going about its work although we were loafing in gilded idleness.

The cruising steamers had gone and so too the many-hued coaches which had taken visitors on bus trips before the war. Of an afternoon, at an hour which happily coincided with a slack period for steamers, we sat on a low white wall at the top of the gardens in Marine Parade and watched the motor-coaches go off from Dunoon to Inveraray, Loch Eck, Puck's Glen, Glendaruel, Glen Masson and a whole gazeteer of other places. Every bus was as individual to us as a living creature. Hartley's was the Silver Line and its coaches were old for the most part, charabancs, really, but lovingly maintained. Some were open, some enclosed, but each carried the prefix Silver in its name, and again blue blood was stressed: Silver Knight, Silver Countess, Silver Baron and so on. Baird's coaches were blue and fairly anonymous but a third line had a dashing chocolate-and-yellow livery. Its coaches were covered, had a clock behind the driver's cabin and curtains at the windows, which we thought the last word in sophistication. We accounted their titles of Miss Modern and Miss 1930 very dashing indeed. No more charabancs, and indeed within a couple of years the extremely comfortable local passenger buses which ran between Sandbank and Dunoon had largely been replaced by wartime utility vehicles which had slatted wooden seats that were the ultimate in irksomeness.

Out on the Firth the boom stretched between the Cloch lighthouse and the Gantocks rocks off Gourock. This accounted for the drastic reduction in steamer services, for it was not now possible to sail to such ports as Rothesay and Ayr from Kirn. The great river was busier than ever with convoys assembling off Greenock and a continual scudding of warships. The neutral ships had their flags painted on their hulls and a large light which they trained on their colours while at sea. There were still neutral ships about in 1940, notably Swedish and Greek vessels, to say nothing of the Americans.

My mother had the looking-after of us as my father could only manage down on Sundays and his arrival by steamer at 11 o'clock was the event of the week. A wartime bonus was that Kirn pier now opened on Sunday whereas before only Dunoon had functioned on the Sabbath. In the afternoon or early evening he would take us out in one of Reggie Brooks' rowing boats and I never venerated him more than when he sat, sports jacket discarded and in shirt-sleeves, effortlessly whisking us out from the low, rubber-tyred jetty over the near-shore rocks to the white sand that so surprisingly gleamed only 20 yards further out. He had to catch the early morning Monday steamer back and was sometimes away before we were stirring but although the trip must often have been an additional burden at the end of a heavy week, it was one that he never failed to make throughout the wartime years.

If there was a rainy evening we went to the Kozy Korner in Dunoon where there was a summer show with Bert Bendon as comic. I cannot remember anything he did and it is strange that his name should have stuck. I do recall a soubrette, Edith Thompson, who sang a faintly risqué song, "Me and my dog, just lost in the fog, won't some kind gentleman take us home?" In the Castle Gardens in Dunoon the war song of the moment played by the orchestra at its afternoon sessions was *The Navy's Here* which commemorated the taking off of British merchant seamen from the German prison ship *Altmark* and was as inspired as such songs usually are.

Eventually it was time to re-pack the trunk and we said our fare-wells to those local boys with whom we had renewed acquaintance after missing out on the summer before. We returned our battered and increasingly loose-leafed novels to the lending library and without enthusiasm boarded the *Marchioness of Lorne* for the return crossing to Gourock. In normal times we would have sailed up the river on the *Kylemore* or *Eagle III*. When we had done that we had been able to kid ourselves that we were going on a cruise, at least we could until we passed Dumbarton Rock. Calling at Renfrew and Govan disabused us of that notion as the river grew murkier by the second and the smell more noxious. We would in those easier days see our first Glasgow tram for a month just before we puzzled over a pungent and imperfectly grasped piece of advice to His Holiness on the cranes of Harland and Wolff's shipyard.

Now in 1940, the tubby little *Marchioness* threaded her way among the towering merchantmen and warships which lay off Gourock. We changed trains at the Central Station, took the Cathcart Circle for Mount Florida to find that my grandmother or Aunt Julia would have tea ready for us. We then clattered out for an hour or so to see which of our pals were back in circulation and had remembered us.

The police had remembered me, or at any rate my paper round. When I reported back for duty it was to be told that inquiries had been made about my age and that I was four years short of the minimum age for delivery, I would have to go. I was savagely annoyed at this but by the time the police caught up with my illegal occupation and I was politely warned off, I had saved enough for my bicycle. It was an inexpensive conveyance for there had been a run on new bicycles in the wake of the French surrender and even 18-inch ones had disappeared. I had therefore to make do with a second-hand one, which I purchased for 15 shillings. I invested as much again for new pedals, hand grips, brake blocks and one or two odds and ends like a bell, a lamp and a pump. The next problem was to learn how to "go" my bike (nobody ever "rode" a bike in Mount Florida). I managed this by the proven expedient of persevering until my falls became less frequent and in time ceased altogether.

With the acquisition of the new bike my horizons were extended. I pushed out beyond Busby to East Kilbride and in breaking this new ground I received a bizarre injury when a horse chestnut fell from a tree and laid the bridge of my nose open. Before winter closed in I sometimes took the bike to school, since doing so gave me a precious extra ten minutes in the house at lunch time, or, as we called it, dinner time.

School was now back in full swing and I was in the Qualifying Class, performance in which would determine whether I went on to secondary school or remained behind in Holy Cross in what was euphemistically called the Advanced Division. My teacher came from Motherwell and Miss Rita Hepburn believed that small boys and girls were there to be taught. She made not the slightest concession to the war, did not stoop to notice its existence, and we did mental arithmetic, spellings and the analysis of sentences until they came out of our ears. It was repetitive, rote work, demanding . . . and superb teaching because the questing spirit was also encouraged. There was a ten-minute topic spell every day wherein we could get our red herrings safely out of the way.

The late summer of 1940 was dominated, so far as the news bulletins were concerned, by the Battle of Britain but although we cheered every announcement of our victories, including the literally fabulous account of the 185 German planes destroyed in a day, the battle was far off for the Scots. We evolved a complicated game on bicycles which we called Spitfires and Heinkels, the nub of which was that if you managed to get within a certain distance of the other bike from behind, you were deemed to have shot him down. We weaved in and out of the increasingly traffic-free streets, imitating machine-gun fire, and no doubt made thorough nuisances of ourselves.

Petrol was beginning to run short and questions were asked about the number of afternoon race meetings and greyhound meetings. Looking back, it seems incredible that these went on at a time of national crisis but in sober truth there were more than a million unemployed in Britain in the month of Dunkirk. There was no call for masses of untrained men to be used as cannon fodder as there had been in 1914.

We were more vexed by the fact that football would not be getting back to a pre-war footing, although had it done so our beloved Queen's Park would have been consigned to the Second Division. As it was there was now no Second Division but although our side remained in the top rank, we felt this was not compensated for by the loss of such as Aberdeen, Kilmarnock, Ayr United and Queen of the South, all of whom closed down on account of the war. Even in football there were interesting local variations. Most of the Glasgow district junior clubs kept going but Cambuslang Rangers disbanded in 1940 because Cambuslang was a keen Territorial Army town and had suffered considerable losses in France in the early summer.

On Sundays there were military bands in the Queen's Park and during the week concert parties. Although the bands played military music most of the time, there was usually a spot where they played popular tunes of the day. There were instrumental soloists of course who played pieces like the *Post Horn Gallop* and anything else which was designed to display their expertise in triple-tonguing, and there was also a vocalist who would be a carbon copy of Len Camber or Al Bowly or any of the British crooners of the time. One such vocalist showed great misjudgement or perhaps courage in electing to sing *There'll always be an England*, never the most popular of songs with a Scottish audience. The last verse was totally inaudible against a background of derisive shouts and hooting.

Much more to the taste of the groundlings was the song given by a member of a concert party some weeks later. In those days the compére normally wore evening dress no matter the time of performance and the number of the item was displayed on stands at the side of the stage so that the audience could consult their programmes and see that they were getting value for money. In the Queen's Park many got value for no money at all since they leaned over the hedge at the back of the auditorium and had a completely uninterrupted view. These "hedge sparrows" as they were known, were in raptures at the performance of the senior female member of the concert party who emerged as a hard-bitten Glasgow housewife, a "targe" in local idiom, to deliver the following song. Two score years have failed to blur its awfulness and I remember it word for word

> Send for Fanny, good old Fanny,
> Good old Fanny McIntyre,
> Ah'm only a workin' woman
> An' no' a bloomin' toff
> Ah could slaughter a' the Jerries noo
> If Ah only had a wee hauf.
> Send for Fanny, good old Fanny,
> The girl they all admire
> And there's nothin' Ah widnae do
> For the old red, white and bue *(Produces flag from cleavage)*
> Good old Fanny McIntyre.

The audience loved it and I suppose it was no worse than *There'll always be an England.*

Early in October 1940 my sister Kathleen was born. We boys had not the remotest idea that my mother was expecting and on the day that she went into hospital we were looked after by my grandmother. This was a clever move because had we been sent to Bill's mother, our Aunt Betty, the penny might have dropped. We had gone there in November 1938 and the result had been my sister Julie. We came to love Julie in a very short space of time but our enthusiasm on being told of her birth was, it is fair to say, tepid. We simply could not understand why our parents were so delighted and to Philip's question "What use is a girl?" we received no satisfactory answer.

She seemed in fact to present one immediate hindrance, as we were compelled to take her for walks in her new pram. It was quite impossible for our walks not to take us in the direction of the Recreation Ground because our friends had not ceased to play football because we had a new sister. Most great scientific discoveries are happened upon rather than consciously sought and I cannot remember which of us found out that a pram made a stable and visible goal-post much superior to our normal coat or jacket and rather less likely to be left behind. We always turned the hood of the pram towards the playing area so it could not be said that we were entirely heartless.

Even then I believed in making the best of things. My sister's name was Julie, which with a little adaptation could become Julia, the name of my current *inamorata* in Primary Four. I told her authoritatively on the day my sister was born that we had named the new-born infant after her. She was suitably gratified and for a time our relationship prospered. The coming of a second sister was to bring great changes to all our lives, had we but known it.

On the day of the christening, I had taken an early breakfast and gone to church equally early. Then with a couple of sandwiches in my saddle-bag, a recent acquisition, I set off without telling anyone where I was going. I was going to Kilmarnock but knew that if I disclosed this I would not be allowed to do so. On my diminutive bike I climbed the long, slow hill to Newton Mearns and set off across the bleakness of the Fenwick Moor. There was little to see except the windmill pumps whirring round near the isolated farm-houses and the occasional convoy of heavy lorries driven by soldiers under instruction. After a short stop in the village of Fenwick I reached the outskirts of Kilmarnock and enquired of a returning churchgoer the location of Rugby Park, home of Kilmarnock Football Club. On being given this information I went there, thinking of other words for going, such as "proceeding" or "repairing" and in the street outside the ground ate my corned beef sandwiches. The ground was closed on a Sunday, of course, and as a football ground it was to remain closed for the next five years as it had been taken

over for the installation of petrol tanks. It mattered not. I had seen
the ground with its round-roofed Dutch barn-type grandstand and
from now on when the grown-ups talked of past matches there, I
could put scene to story.

The journey back was grim. I was tired in any event and the wind
was strongly in my face. Unusually for that time of year it must have
been coming out of the north. I had just enough energy to reach
Newton Mearns, from where it was happily downhill all the way. I
cheered up at the prospect of the special tea there would be in
connection with the christening and the fact that my Aunt Julia and
Uncle Joe would be there, with one or two other relatives that we
also liked. I was within half a mile of home in the fast-gathering
darkness (I had misjudged the time, which had added to the troubles
of the homeward leg) when the front wheel of my bicycle caught in
the tram rails and threw me from the saddle. I was winded but not at
all hurt and there was just enough blood in evidence to be gratifying.
Tired but achieving, I carried the offending vehicle on my shoulder
up the stairs to our first-floor flat. I was nonchalantly sponging my
cut leg in the bathroom when my father came in and told me that our
family had outgrown Clincart Road and that we would have to leave
Mount Florida.

Much later in life, I often stayed my hand against my own
children when I recollected my father's astonishing forbearance
with me. At ten years of age I should have been a staff and prop to
my parents at this time. I was not, and worse, attempted to suborn
Frank and Philip who were of a more sensible disposition. There
was no question of our leaving the Mount. What would we do for
friends? Make new ones, it was suggested. Our riposte that we didn't
want new friends was disregarded. What about the danger to our
schooling, was my next crafty suggestion? The parents had thought
of that and instituted divide and rule. I could stay where I was at
Holy Cross, since I was so near to sitting the Qualifying examination, the others would have to change quarters.

We were not appeased. We held a council of action and canvassed
the possibilities of running away. Strangely, on this the youngest
brother, Philip, was the acknowledged expert. Periodically he
would make ferocious assaults on Frank, with whom he lived at all
other times in the utmost amity. Threatened with being sent to the
Bad Boys' Home he would shout "Right!" with great decision and
go off to throw some things in a case. He then stormed out of the
house and while he normally stood in full view under the nearest gas

lamp waiting for a recall from his distraught parents, he had on occasion reached the end of the street.

There was a tree in the Recreation Ground which we thought might serve, for we used it as a den and there was a bush behind it to act as wind-break. But could we light a fire at night in the black-out? Probably not, we decided. We hinted to Bill's mother that we would be prepared to come and stay with her and that we were very good at going messages, as she knew, but there were no takers. It was bundle and pack. Neither Julie's second birthday party nor Christmas could console us and as the first great air raids of the war rained bombs on London and Coventry we were suffering our own form of shell-shock.

Chapter Four

1941:
When the buds peep through the snow

NO matter our depth of feeling, there could be no doubt that my father was right when he said that the house in Clincart Road was not big enough for us. The wonder, indeed, was that it had sufficed for the last four years, even before the arrival of Kathleen. We lived in a first-floor flat in a good red sandstone tenement, a type of building in which Glasgow abounded and which at its best could fairly claim to be one of the finest forms of European urban housing. We had a kitchen — the flat was basically what was known as a room and kitchen — and this kitchen was used for eating and had a recess bed in the style which was common to the time. Off the kitchen was a microscopic scullery where the cooking was done and the dishes washed up. There was just about enough room for a person of slim build to turn to the stove from the sink but it was quite impossible for more than one person to work there at a time.

There was a fairly large hall or lobby which was totally disproportionate to the size of the house and from it led doors to the sitting room, which also contained a double recess bed, and to the long, narrow, cold bathroom which completed the apartments of the house. It was a substantial house though small, and situated in a "good" district of Glasgow. The close, or common entrance, was tiled, the decorated banister was of solid wood and the glass panel on our door was of stained glass.

From the windows of "the room", as it was always called, there was a most rewarding prospect. Our house was on the crest of the more southern of the two ridges which gave Mount Florida its name and we were right on the corner of the block. When I looked out, before me were spread the villas of Langside and Newlands, the sedate houses of Old Cathcart, and in the further distance the hills of Renfrewshire and the Cathkin Braes. Indeed, my imagination took me much further since one of the Newlands houses which could be made out was in crenellated Gothic and nothing would satisfy my overheated fancy but that this particular building was Stirling Castle. The road to Carmunnock was in full view and we used to look out for Young's buses which went up to that village and which, with their drab blue livery, seemed very countrified to my young eyes when compared with the more sophisticated green-and-cream buses of Glasgow Corporation Transport Department.

As I say, it was a marvellous view and never more so than when the autumn sou'westers hurled themselves against our corner house, making the windows rattle as I looked out at the gas-lit streets, or watched a train on the Cathcart Circle taking the loop which would lead it out to the newly settled King's Park. There was something oddly comforting in seeing the glowing sparks from the funnel tossed about in the turbulent night and I have never since been able to take a lit bus or train at night for granted.

However we were not to live there any more and as the day of our moving approached we fell into a dull kind of acquiescence. We made one or two sallies to "the new house" although our primary purpose in doing so was to work out the quickest way back to Mount Florida. Responsibility was about to be thrust upon us in no small measure.

A flitting is an upheaval. This is true at any time and much more so during a war, but the circumstances of our move to Shawlands in January 1941 could hardly have been more disruptive. For some time now, my father had been complaining of severe stomach pains and about a week before Christmas he came home early from work at the pub one evening in a state of collapse, to find that, fortunately, my Aunt Julia was there as well as my mother. The doctor had him removed to the Victoria Infirmary where he was found to have a duodenal ulcer. He could be cured by strict adherence to a diet and an operation was not thought necessary but he would have to be hospitalised for a couple of weeks and when he was released there would be no question of an immediate return to work.

I had been up later than usual and was therefore still around when my father came in with his face the colour of parchment. At once I was hustled off the scene but through the wall I could hear the discussion which went on between my parents and my aunt. The first priority had to be the shop, which my father was running on his own with the help of another man who came in at five o'clock every night. Given the wartime shortage of labour it would be quite impossible to get full-time help even if my father had been in the position to take on a full-time employee in a business which was very much still making its way. Quite apart from the economic necessity of keeping the pub, the *Ailsa Craig*, going, it was illegal to close a public house even for holidays without the permission of the magistrates.

My mother reacted with her customary promptness and vigour. She would herself take over the running of the *Ailsa Craig*. All my father's protests about her total inexperience, the unsuitability of the job for a woman, her own indifferent health, the short time since the arrival of Kathleen, were swept aside. Before he was taken off to hospital he dictated a long list of do's and don'ts which my mother faithfully transcribed. On her way to open up the pub the following morning, she was reading them over in the tram when, as she got up to alight, in her agitation she threw the list of instructions into the used-ticket receptacle and for the rest of the day she had to operate from memory.

The second problem was us. Who would look after five children ranging from myself at ten to Kathleen at two months? Once more my grandmother was pressed into that service from which in truth she had never escaped. For the remaining nine years of her life, at a time when she had some justifiable expectation of leisure, she made the journey every day by public transport between her house and ours to cook, clean and wash for us.

By the time my father was discharged from hospital it was also time to leave the Mount. The removal took place in my mother's absence with my father supervising but unable to do any heavy lifting. In terms of distance it was not a long removal, a little under two miles I would suppose. Our new house lay on the other side of the steep Langside Monument Hill and we made several trips between the two addresses. In the cold, raw January afternoon Frank and myself manfully pushed the pram which contained an assortment of household odds and ends up the long gradual slope to Battlefield Monument. As we passed the Victoria Infirmary we could see the windows of the ward where my father had been only a few days before. Then we reached the summit and plunged down the side of the Queen's Park, the heavy pram threatening to drag our feeble arms from their sockets. My father had gone on ahead with the removers and the three youngest children had been taken over in a taxi by their grandmother, to our outspoken envy.

In all, we made three round trips on one of those days, typical of the early new year in Scotland, when there is such an iron frost that snow would come as a relief. We groped our way through the dusk to number 207 Deanston Drive, unloaded our final cargo and then set about organising a meal. Here we had blundered badly by forgetting provisions. Food was by now quite stringently rationed and we were still registered with shops in Mount Florida. I was dispatched to touch the hearts of the Shawlands shopkeepers and persuade them to let us have a little food off the ration. I failed lamentably, despite growing practise in reciting our harrowing tale. Closing time drew nearer and still no shopkeeper was sufficiently taken with my blandishments to risk the prosecution by the Ministry of Food that a generous impulse might bring. Finally, a young girl in a grocer's shop let me have half a pound of cheese and the same quantity of margarine. On that, and a tin of unrationed cocoa, we made our first meal in the new home.

In some respects, though not all, the new home was more imposing than the one we had just left. The close mouth was distinctly workaday and we had a ground-floor flat, on the left-hand side. At the end of the long narrow hall the living-room, a new term for us, was half-right. We noticed at once that it had a built-in larder, a display cabinet and a good solid book-case. There were two bedrooms and a lounge and the bedroom allocated to the three boys had a gas fire. This was luxury and also fearfully unrealistic as the bars of the gas fire were very fragile and soon suffered substantial casualties.

In place of the Lilliputian scullery of Clincart Road there was a proper kitchenette with a gas cooker and two sinks, one of them very deep and suitable for washing clothes. The wash-house in Mount Florida had been located in the back-green and washing day had started with the lighting of a fire in the boiler and finished with putting clothes through the wringer before hanging them out. The bathroom was small but perfectly adequate and there was a patch of garden at the front about the size of a large Wilton carpet. The front view was a great come-down after the Mount. We looked across the street straight into a row of houses, or, to be more accurate, in January 1941 we looked across the street towards a half-built row of houses.

In the back-green we found air-raid shelters already built to serve our own close, 207, and the next one, 211. Beyond the back-green was a lane wide enough to drive a car down and over the lane were the backs of the houses on Tantallon Road which were privately factored tenements. The names of the families in our close, Crampsey, Edgar, McMahon, McDougall, Beaton, Donaldson, Cassidy and Duffy were almost perversely typical of the amalgam of Highland, Lowland and Irish that is Glasgow.

I suppose that my parents saw it as a lateral social move, if they thought of that aspect at all, since Shawlands was highly esteemed as a residential district. On our side of the street there had apparently been some vetting of potential tenants and this was intended for the housing development as a whole. In the event, the houses opposite were given to those bombed out in the heavy air-raids of the next few months, many of the new arrivals coming from Tradeston and Anderston. My mother and some of the ladies on our side of the street tended to deplore this, my father to take the more realistic view that refugees had to live somewhere and why not Deanston Drive? His opinion may well have been swayed by the fact that Anderston had provided him with a home for several years after his arrival in Glasgow. As for us, ability to play football was the beginning and end of our attempts at social classification. If a boy could play football, no amount of parental disapproval would stop us associating with him. If he couldn't play or, even worse, was uninterested no amount of advocacy was capable of making us regard him with favour. Most of the good players lived across the road so that settled that.

It was a long time before our house was anything like as well equipped as my mother would have wished. Woman-like, she took the niggling shortages of wartime harder than the arduous task of having to run the *Ailsa Craig*. She was doing well in Scotland Street; she had always had a good business head and the customers were extremely helpful in what could have been a very trying situation. Kinning Park was not the most urbane district of Glasgow but in a pub with no pretensions it was virtually unheard of for anyone to treat her with anything but marked courtesy and a certain formality.

As had been promised, I remained at Holy Cross School since I would qualify within a few months. My brothers were transferred to the strangely named St Conval's School, strange because it had a Pictish tower and because it did not share its name with the church next door which was St Mary's. The parish priest at the time was a handsome, florid Irishman, Canon Ned Lawton, whose picture had appeared in the peacetime newspapers, normally at Ayr races or Hamilton or wherever the meeting was, to the scandalising of one half of his flock and the delight of the other.

St Conval's was in Pollokshaws which in the 1940s still retained many of the characteristics of a village, indeed there was still the very occasional house with an earthen floor. I was intrigued by my brothers' accounts of their new schoolfellows, particularly by their tales of the Ferguson family, extremely large and unruly and where the children came alternately into the world as blonds and redheads. The White Fergies and The Red Fergies became part of my everyday imaginings and many years later my friend Pat Harrigan, greatly irked by some loutish behaviour on the part of a White Fergie, turned him into a red one by the simple process of emptying a bottle of ink over him.

I travelled back to Crosshill every day by train on the grimy carriages of the Cathcart Circle. To come to school by rail gave me a certain status, heightened by the fact that Jean, the prettiest girl in the class, now lived at 211 and we travelled back and forward together. For the next six years I hurled myself up the dank stairs of Pollokshaws East station for the 8.49 a.m. trying to avoid breathing in the noisome smell of the gas lamps. Many a morning or lunch hour, judging things too finely, I would be half running alongside, half dragged by, the moving train until eventually I could wrench open the heavy-handled carriage door, sink down on the cushions and not draw breath until Cathcart, two stations down the line. Still it was grand to go by train and have a quarterly season ticket and keep it in a real wallet. I could also keep the school friends I had.

The war made very little difference to our primary school teaching. It meant an additional prayer every day for peace and we prayed a lot. We had prayed for Pius XI in the winter of 1939 but he had died just the same. Religion was pervasive in the school day but never oppressive, and if I was now a frontiersman, travelling in from Shawlands, in truth I had always been that because when we lived in Mount Florida there would hardly be half a dozen other Catholic families there. The main difference between my schooling and that of my Mount Florida friends, who to a man went to the primary school of the same name, was that they had a week longer for their summer holidays to make up for our Holidays of Obligation which were dotted about the calendar, often falling, to our fury, on a Saturday or Sunday.

There was a lot of rote learning of course but we were also continually being told about what was going on in the world out- side. In the best Scottish democratic tradition the intake of the school was very wide-ranging. At one pole there were the doctors' children and the lawyers' children of Queen's Drive, Queen Mary Avenue and Myrtle Park. Even more exotic was the lovely, fluffy, blonde girl whose father had fought for the middleweight championship of the world and lost. Before Hitler, she arrived every morning in a chauffeur-driven limousine and as she passed my house on the way I was often given a lift to the school gate. At the other extreme there were the children from Robson Street and Old Polmadie, half a mile and a world away. In the late 1930s there were several in the class who received their clothes from "the parish", their garb being distinguishable by its uniformity and by the heaviness of the boots. The clothes did not differ too much in style from those of the more affluent boys, even at the outbreak of war. The woollen jersey and matching tie were the order of the day although the parents of one boy, fortunately tall, well set-up and brave, dispatched him to school in a sailor suit.

Our education was based on the principle that if the basics were hammered they would become second nature and there would be time for more interesting things if not necessarily more important things. We had long since left counters and the early reader which began with the sentence "Will the dog go to Nell?" aside. One of the Robson Street boys, who was actually important enough to have a brother in Borstal, yelled out during one interval, "Will the dog go to Nell? Will it hell!" We looked on, astounded that he was not struck dead on the spot.

There was a lot of striking dead on the spot. Miss Hepburn told us of the woman in London who had seized the chance provided by the confusion of an air-raid to steal a purse from one of the victims. She had been spotted, taxed with the crime, vehemently denied it — "May God strike me down dead if I took that purse" — and on cue, fell in a crumpled heap and, said Miss Hepburn fiercely, "out rolled the purse from her jacket!" We were appalled and spent the next few hours returning a myriad of things which we had purloined.

We had air-raid drill, supervised by the headmaster, Mr McCrossan, a tall, lean man who did not look pompous but was, and his short, fat assistant Mr Kelly, who looked pompous and was not. We called him, out of hearing, Mr Kettlebelly, with a wary eye for the avenging bolt. Our games had changed. Cigarette cards were no longer being issued, so that we could not now play "face or a blank?", a simple but absorbing game. For this your opponent held his cards concealed in a doubled fist. You said to him "two a face" or "seven a blank" as you thought best. If he had been holding the cards upwards in the first instance, that is with the picture showing, he gave you two and if the writing was on top then you paid up.

Holy Cross School offered a form of education which was particularly suited to a newspaper-reading infant like myself. Prayers for peace were not anything new in our school and had been the occasion of my greatest monetary triumph to date. In the July of 1936 the Spanish Civil War broke out and just after our return to school in August our class was visited by Miss Macdonald, the Infants Mistress.

"I want you all to pray very hard for peace in Spain, children," she said. "There is a terrible war there although of course you will not know about that."

"Please miss, I know all about it," I said nauseatingly.

"Indeed, Robert?" She was one of the few people who ever called me by my given name. "Then suppose you tell us what kind of war it is?"

"Please, miss, it's a civil war."

"And what does that mean?"

"Please miss, two sides from the same country." While she hesitated, no doubt impressed, I followed up. "Please miss, one of the sides is called the Government".

"And the other one?"

"The insurgents." Always willing to give value for money I added, "Some people call them the Nationalists".

"And I suppose you know who their leader is?"

"Please, miss, one of their leaders is General Franco. He is trying to capture Madrid."

"And how far away is he?"

"Twenty-one miles yesterday. He does about three miles a day."

Miss Macdonald had heard more than enough. Out of admiration for my virtuosity, or, as I now think, to shut me up at any price, she reached into her purse and handed me tuppence wordlessly. I had never in my life been given twopence before and the problem of disposing of this sum was totally baffling. I had not resolved it when I returned to Mount Florida after four o'clock and met Archie who was a friend but not a particularly close friend. We discussed how we might spend this money and eventually could think of nothing more constructive than to buy several boxes of matches and go up to the Rock, which lay on the path between Mount Florida railway station and Battlefield. We used the Rock as a vantage point to watch incoming trains when we were playing Indians and we now tried to set the railway embankment on fire, a task in which we were highly unsuccessful. My feat of brilliance did me no good whatever as of course Miss Macdonald had recounted the conversation to my Aunt Julia in the staff room. She in turn told my mother who thereupon wanted to know what had happened to the money.

But that had been long ago and in the early spring of 1941 I, with the rest of the class, parsed, analysed, did ten "mental" each morning, did ten spellings each morning and a monthly "Big Test In Ink", all with a view to passing the "Qually". In the lighter February days it was time to look around and see what kind of a domain we had inherited with our new address. It was not without promise. There were three cinemas to hand, the Embassy, the Elephant and the Waverley, and although we were not fanatical cinema-goers, they were useful to have in reserve in case there was a long spell of bad weather which would prevent us from going to Cathkin or Hampden. A few hundred yards away lay the Bluebell Woods which we identified at a glance as having great possibilities for sledging and perhaps even greater possibilities for getting one's head stoved in as the track swerved round trees and finally plunged through a narrow hummocky gap in a blackthorn hedge. The woods were also excellent terrain for tracking, a game to which we had been introduced by Billy Edgar, who lived across the close and who, although not interested in football, was a good lad and very adept at tracking. He promised to make us as skilled at it as he was.

The half-finished houses opposite provided a handy playground. We raided them frequently when the watchman was distracted and stole small lengths of wood which we fashioned into swords. With these we enacted scenes from such films as *The Sea Hawk*, which allowed some athletic duels in the manner of Errol Flynn engaging Basil Rathbone, and *Bitter Sweet* which did not. I had always liked the duel sequence in *Bitter Sweet* in which George Sanders disposed of Nelson Eddy in about five seconds flat. It seemed to me exactly what would have happened in real life as Nelson Eddy was clearly not one of nature's swordsmen.

We had run through our fencing repertoire one evening in March, gone back in and were having the gruel-like cocoa when the sirens went and almost immediately afterwards the guns opened up and bombs began to fall, although not particularly near. In a short while it became clear that this was a raid of an unparalleled severity and we dived beneath the stout living room table. There seemed to be a collective decision not to go to the shelter. Many people who decided otherwise would not be alive come the morning.

By ten o'clock the bombing had intensified. We began to be greatly worried about my father who had not come home and my grandmother abandoned all thoughts of going back to Kinning Park that evening. My father got in about midnight with the news that there had been some heavy bombing down near Eglinton Street although the tramcars were still running on his particular route. The next morning we learned indirectly from a boy whose father was in the Fire Service that Clydebank had been largely destroyed. The raid had been most severe but it was the repetition on the same scale the following night that really shook people. It began to seem as if Glasgow would be in the same position as London with heavy raids for weeks and perhaps months on end.

I cannot recall that we were in the least frightened during the raids. The adults were clearly the more worried because they had a much starker vision of possible consequences. As often as not, especially if there was no action following the variable sound of the alert, but even if there was, we were more concerned with the passage of time. The rule affecting school attendance stipulated that if a raid lasted until midnight then pupils need not attend until the following afternoon and if it extended until one o'clock in the morning then they need not attend at all on the following day. We found ourselves in the position of encouraging the Luftwaffe to stay up there until the appointed hour, forgetful or careless of the fact that property was being damaged and lives possibly lost.

Evacuation once again became a distinct possibility. My mother had cousins who lived in Neilston, a small Renfrewshire town about ten miles away, and it was seriously suggested that we should go and live there. The three boys set to work on my father and told him we were heroically determined to die in the breach with our parents. I was heroically determined to do something and offered my services as a messenger boy to the Civil Defence authorities. In my mind's eye I saw myself on my bicycle dodging through the debris-strewn streets to deliver messages "of vital import" as Dixon Hawke and Sexton Blake were wont to say. I was commended for my public zeal and told to apply again in three years or so.

We stayed where we were but had to promise my father that we would go out to the shelter the moment that the sirens sounded the warning. This was the seven-arched brick structure in the back green with two families sharing each compartment. Any security it provided was at best psychological since the shelters were hastily thrown-up brick constructions. Ours was always cold and dank and attempts to make it more cheerful only served to intensify the gloom. We hung mats across the door, not only to keep out the cold but to allow us to light torches and storm lamps. We carried out chairs and sat in the weird light, jerkins and trousers pulled over pyjamas. We drank tea and ate sandwiches of the bread which was growing steadily darker as the war progressed. We were horribly fascinated by our first blitzed tenement with its great baulks of timber, glass everywhere and a bath perched precariously on the ruined third floor, lurching drunkenly against the still-bright pattern of the wallpaper. The raids were to continue for fully another year but with one exception we were never to be greatly threatened.

Whenever possible we went back to Mount Florida to play with our pals of long standing, indeed there was a sense in which we always thought of ourselves as Mount boys. This was not always practicable, however, particularly on a Saturday morning when we had to get in the messages—they were always messages, never errands—before being free to go over the hill. By the time we arrived play had invariably started and although our credit was good enough to get us on either side "cock or a hen", Phil acting as make-weight for Frank, we were imposing on the good nature of the players.

We therefore, while keeping in close contact with Bill, had a look at what alliances we might make on the spot. Shawlands was not quite the hot-bed of football that Mount Florida had been and few boys shared our mania for the game but there were two who were keen. One was a good-looking, curly, dark-haired lad called Bobby Devlin who would be dead within four years and the other was a tall, stooped boy called Georgie Miller who in everyday life had a face as chalk-white as that of a fully made-up circus clown. George was a Partick Thistle supporter, the first one that we had ever met to talk to, living as we did on the south side of the river. They were not particularly numerous on the north side either.

We had discovered junior football, a strange semi-professional grade which flourished nowhere else bar in Scotland and the ground of Pollok Juniors lay only a few hundred yards away beyond the River Cart. By this stage in the war professional senior players trained when and where they could and there were often players from the big clubs at Newlandsfield of an evening. At a somewhat later period of the war, we went along to the Pollok ground one evening but without Georgie, who was taking part in a Boys' Brigade display. One of George's Partick Thistle idols, Maurice Candlin, was training and as we reached our close on the way home we met George, also returning, pill-box hat on head, polished belt on shoulder. Like true friends we hastened to acquaint him with what he had missed.

"You should have been there tonight, Georgie. Maurice Candlin was at Newlandsfield training."

"Wis Maurice therr?" asked Georgie, pale face crumpled with chagrin.

"He was."

"Wis he kickin' the ba'?" Riches beyond belief.

"He was."

"That must have been some sight." And off went honest George up the stairs, disconsolate, like some soldier of the Old Guard who had just failed to snatch a glimpse of the Emperor at Grenoble in the "Hundred Days".

May saw some heavy raids on Greenock which meant that we were not yet out of the evacuation wood. Neilston was again proposed and rejected. Suddenly the ARP regulations which had seemed irksome and futile made sense. An Ayrshire farm-hand who shone his unscreened torch into the sky was given 60 days in which to contemplate the folly of his action while there were reports from the courts of looters at Clydebank being given up to 18 months imprisonment, sentences which the public felt to be disturbingly lenient. As the war struck harder, public tolerance of those who were damaging the war effort or civilian morale, understandably waned.

We beat off the Neilston threat yet again, although since one of my aunt's daughters was getting married and leaving home there would have been room for us. To show that there was no ill-feeling on our part I volunteered to take my cousin's wedding present out to her—towels, I well remember. I remember too that almost all the time I was there she kept singing *I'll be with you in apple blossom time* which got on my nerves, although the poor girl was only showing a very natural happiness.

I got back from Neilston to hear our hottest news of the war to date. Rudolf Hess had fled from Germany and landed in a field near Eaglesham, scarcely ten miles away. The Home Guard, who had been the subject of many jokes, had been early on the scene here and very naturally made the most of it. Their delight and consequent self-importance knew no bounds. It transpired later on that Hess had flown from Augsburg in a Messerschmidt 110E in search of the Duke of Hamilton's estate at Dungavel, and had performed a superb feat of navigation in a plane which was alien to him. Judging by the numbers of our friends who claimed to have a piece of the 110E in the weeks that followed, it must have been of something approaching the dimensions of the modern Boeing 747.

We didn't know why Hess had come. It was all a bit of a mystery and the Government sat on the story for some considerable time, although we were titillated by the news that while awaiting permanent captivity he had read Jerome K. Jerome's *Three Men in a Boat* twice. The speed with which war stories were released varied greatly. A few weeks later the sinking of HMS *Hood*, an undeniable disaster since she was the largest warship in the world and only three members of her crew survived from a ship's complement of more than 1300, was made known at once and not infrequently the names of victims of small-scale air-raids were released immediately.

The great event of the early summer of 1941 was, of course, the invasion of Russia. It was rather overshadowed for me by the sitting of the Qualifying Examination which had taken place a few days earlier. The examination was for a total of 160 marks and when, in company with two others, I returned 155 I felt fairly pleased with life and modestly prepared to receive my meed of due praise from the Headmaster, Mr McCrossan. I did not then regard his muttered "Disappointing, Crampsey" as the kind of inverted compliment I suppose that it was. We formed a small class committee and, under our own steam, took a collection and a morning off. We went into town and bought a reasonably presentable handbag for Miss Rita Hepburn who had served us well. The Holy Cross days were almost over.

The Russian ones were just beginning. There was a definite quickening of tempo in the war after the invasion on 23 June 1941. This was partly because a substantial number of people who had been holding back the wagon now began to shove it, at the same time shouting vociferously. Suddenly, walls were covered with a new slogan, Second Front Now, and what had been a conflict of imperialisms became a holy crusade. There was an official reluctance at first to have much to do with the Soviets. For some time afterwards the Russian national anthem was not included among those played at the end of broadcasting each day and when questions were asked about the omission in the House, the response was that the Russians were not Allies in that sense.

The popular surge more than made up for such omissions. With the promptness that ever distinguishes Tin Pan Alley, pro-Russian songs were on the street by the end of the week. The *Patrol of the Cossack Cavalry* was an early starter but the one that stayed the distance was *Russian Rose*, which had a tune sufficiently strong to carry the banality of the lyrics:

> He will come and find you, break the chains that bind you
> When the buds peep through the snows,
> You will surely bloom again
> My lovely Russian rose.

Stalin was presented as two different people. He at once became Joe, or Uncle Joe, kindly, shrewd, twinkling, while in his other *persona* he was said to have a tremendous liking for Tschaikowsky's *Queen of Spades*. My own family's reaction was probably not untypical: it was better to have them with us than against us, and it was remembered how nearly they had been against us in the Finnish War of 1939-40. At the time of the Finns' surrender permission was being sought of Norway to send a British Expeditionary Force through that country.

The war was still far from going well. The *Bismarck* had been sunk but it had taken half the Royal Navy to do it and although Haile Selassie was back in Addis Abbaba, we had been badly worsted in Greece and Crete. The Government was very anxious that the Germans should not be invested with supernatural powers but it was hard not to notice that when confronted with Italians the Allies were very successful and that when the Germans came along this success terminated abruptly. The Greeks had given the Italian armies a considerable hiding and we were in high hopes that King Zog might be restored to the throne of Albania. Zog had two things going for him. One was his name which was gloriously like that of the subject people of Killer Kane in the *Flash Gordon* serial at the Saturday matinees. These, known as Zugs, had been reduced to a state of total subservience by having an electric helmet placed on their heads which had the effect of rendering them incapable of doing anything but responding to the commands of Killer Kane. We sometimes felt that Hitler had got hold of one of these helmets, or more probably Mussolini had, and forced it upon the luckless monarch Zog. Not totally luckless though because in an age when the newspapers filled pages with accounts of beautiful princesses, most of whom were distinctly homely, Zog's queen, Geraldine, thoroughly merited the title of "beauty". However, the arrival of the Germans in Greece put paid to any thoughts of a speedy restoration of Zog and Geraldine. Zog was inextricably linked in my mind with fish. This was because I had first heard of the Italian invasion of Albania while in McNaughton's fish shop on the morning of Good Friday 1939. I saw him as a man in gorgeous uniform surrounded by fishmongers with red, cold hands, dark-blue and white aprons and straw hats.

No, the Russians were making the news and continued to do so. The *Sunday Pictorial*, not hitherto noted for its commitment to the teaching of modern languages, now instituted a "Teach Yourself Russian" column. Military strategists expended other columns in trying to show that the Red Army which had struggled against the Finns would nevertheless overcome the Wehrmacht and films such as *Russian Salad* had a great vogue. This was a *pot-pourri* of opera, ballet and variety acts and included a marvellously athletic singing of *La Donna e mobile* by a tenor who leapt from a gallery on to a wrought-iron chandelier to make his entrance. This aria was received in respectful attention but a slapstick conductor who hit his own head with his own baton was more to the taste of the audience.

For the only time in the war, we did not go to Kirn in the summer of 1941. My mother had been too busy in the shop to go down to look for accommodation and we now needed a larger house than the one we had used in Argyll Terrace. There was a glorious possibility for a few days or so that we would go to a boarding house called Mount Carmel which would cost all of £20 per week for housing the seven of us. We had never stayed in a boarding house before, indeed had no very clear idea what it was, but we gave ourselves certain airs about this new venture and when it failed to come off our friends quite rightly were highly unsympathetic and gave us a very hard time of it, saying in our hearing, "The Crampsey boys won't be out to play this week, they're away staying in that £20 a week boarding house." Discussion would follow as to whether it was called Mount Carmel or Mount Everest or Mount Florida. We had asked for it and we had to take it. At all events we could console ourselves by the thought that in staying at home we were being very patriotic. Posters were appearing rash-like on every wall asking "Is Your Journey Really Necessary?" and exhorting citizens to "Holiday at Home".

To make the latter proposition more attractive Glasgow Corporation organised shows in the parks and brought carnivals to Glasgow Green and Queen's Park. Senior football too continued virtually the whole year round but these were poor substitutes for the annual visit to Kirn. We did go for a day to Gourock and my poor mother, for whom walking was now increasingly a trial, was perfectly willing to take us over the water but we decided against it and remained on the Renfrewshire side gazing sullenly across the intervening strip of sea.

It was time for me to change schools. The original notion had been that I should sit the entrance examination for St Aloysius' College, a Jesuit-run school right in the centre of Glasgow. The spring bombing had caused my mother to change her mind, and she was the one who took that kind of decision. I was therefore enrolled at Holyrood, a new secondary school much nearer home in Crosshill and the first co-educational Catholic secondary school to be opened in Glasgow. In June I had said good-bye to the Holy Cross of the almost world champion's daughter, of Kettlebelly and Pompous Mac and of the penny catechisms. On 25 August 1941 I walked through the gates of Holyrood Secondary School and gazed beseechingly about for a kent face. Gradually a little knot of Holy Cross boys huddled together and we remained in this attitude of tribal defence until the lines were called in and we were sent to our various classes.

Holyrood was a very modern building, it had been in existence for only five years when I enrolled there. It was a pleasant red-brick structure in the Georgian style and I was impressed by it, and even more by the sight of the masters in their swirling black gowns which I thought to be at once grand and sinister. The playground was extensive and, even after the erection of a large air-raid shelter in the middle of it, comparatively spacious.

Lists were read, groups of pupils departed, including many whom I had taken for adults, until only the first-year entrants were left. There were to be three first-year classes and they were to be called 1A, 1B and 1C in descending academic order. My Qualifying 155 guaranteed me a place with the elect and with 42 others (it was not a particularly exclusive distinction) I went off to a classroom in the wake of a gowned teacher with tufty hair in a quiff and large tortoise-shell spectacles. He was a rather spiky-looking man but within a couple of weeks Mr Moffat had been released from us to join the Royal Navy and we saw him no more.

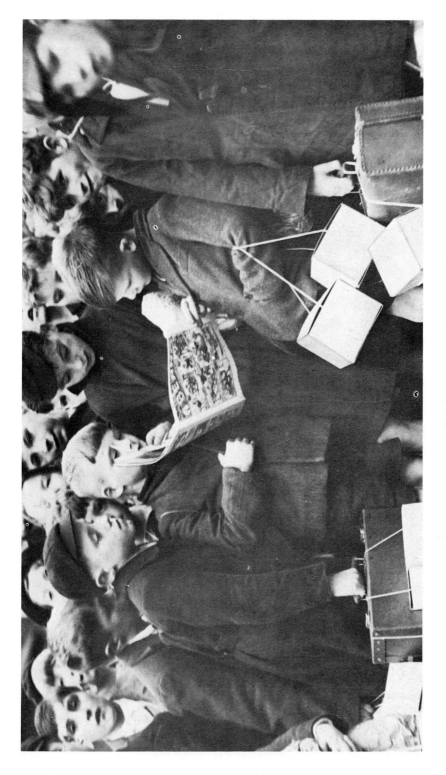

LORD SNOOTY AND HIS FRIENDS

A group of Glasgow primary school children, clutching suitcases and gas mask containers, prepare to evacuate Glasgow in September 1939. Within weeks the great bulk of evacuees had returned to the city.

SALVAGING THE ODDS AND ENDS
Bombed-out families identify their possessions after a raid on Glasgow in April 1941.
Note the brick baffle wall which was supposed to protect the close mouth.

OFF TO A NEW START

The small Glasgow man was the archetype of the industrial West of Scotland. The advances of the Welfare State killed off the flyweights and the bantam battalions.

CLEANING-UP AFTER THE BLITZ
The censor passed this photograph of Clydebank immediately because the tidying-up was good for civilian morale. The absence of wheeled traffic would become ever more noticeable as the war progressed.

HITTING BACK
Two Tommies on returning to the Clyde display surprisingly youthful portraits of Hitler
and Goering following a raid on the Lofoten Islands in 1941.

THE ARRIVAL OF THE DEPUTY FUEHRER

The plane in which Rudolf Hess landed near Eaglesham in May 1941. In weeks to come thousands of West of Scotland boys would claim to have a piece of it as a souvenir.

COMBINED OPS

From the same raid, troops and sailors display a Nazi flag. The Lofoten expedition was comparatively small-scale but good news was scarce and eagerly seized upon.

TO WORK UPON THE RAILWAY

Not Russian but the permanent way just outside Cathcart. This was not the worst of war-time jobs—when the sun shone. By 1942, the date of this picture, the great majority of able-bodied men were with the Forces.

DOLLS' PRAMS AND BARROWS

Home-made transport pressed into service on the chance of some coke from the Tradeston Gas Works. The well-dressed boy wore a corduroy jacket and flying helmet.

LET JOY BE UNCONFINED
Open air dancing for the VE celebrations in the rain.

STREET PARTY

Bunting saved from the 1937 Coronation, and in the case of the big banner, possibly that of 1910.

VJQ

Queues did not disappear with the end of the war. In fact, if anything, they lengthened.

The author and Kathleen at Kirn in the summer of 1942. Folded arms were compulsory for would-be footballers.

Wedding of my Aunt Julia and Uncle Joe, September 1941. Frank and Philip appear bottom left, author bottom right still with arms folded!

My maternal grandfather and namesake, Robert McNaughton.

My maternal grandmother who looked after the family for much the greater part of the war.

Our favourite young Aunt, Julia, with our Cousin Maureen, at Kirn in 1944. The dog, Monty, was a cheerful nondescript mongrel which belonged to us.

My mother, Kitty, as a young woman c.1923.

My parents with Uncle Willie at Kirn just before the war.

The author's sisters, Julie and Kathleen aged approximately five and three.

WILL NO ONE BUY THIS LAD LONG TROUSERS? Fourth year group Holyrood 1945. Pat Hannigan is fifth from left, back row.

I sat at my desk, clad in grey, flannel short trousers and navy-blue blazer. I put my brand-new red notebook, loose-leafed, and my shining yellow and black HB pencil, beautifully pointed, on the desk in front of me and surveyed my new classmates. I already knew more than a dozen of them who had come up with me from Holy Cross. There were others from assorted primary schools, St John's, St Francis, St Mary's, St Vincent's. There were even one or two from outlying districts such as Kennishead, Nitshill and Eaglesham which had not yet been sucked within the Glasgow boundary and the speech of these lads fell very rustically on our ears. Since Holy Cross had the biggest pressure group I was elected class censor and it became my job to convey our attendance figures to our form teacher, Mr Rogers, at various times of the day, thereby ensuring that I quickly became acquainted with the lay-out of the school.

All was strange, all was novelty. The day was divided into nine periods, and after the primary school immurement in one room, it was delightful to move quarters as many times as five in the day. We marvelled in our artless way at the well-equipped gymnasia, the showers, the laboratories, the Geography Room with its fitted maps and the Lecture Room. We soon learned that the great compensation of secondary school was that no teacher, however obnoxious we might find him or her, was master of our spirits for more than two periods together.

The comparative normality of our education was little less than miraculous, given its historical background. There were few young men teachers about and there would be fewer but we did not notice this much, having come from the overwhelmingly female influence of the primary school. We saw the Headmaster, Francis Graham, small, bald, from afar and hoped things would remain so. The older boys told us that "The Dog" was fierce. He had held a commission in the First World War and we strove anxiously to keep out of his way, something we managed without undue difficulty since he very properly did not see us as one of his priorities. We got on with the business of making new friends and I quickly grew to like Pat Harrigan who was humorous and laconic although no games player and Matt Davidson and "Deuce" McSorley who were clearly the best two footballers in the class, with Kenny O'Donnell being the third. They were so good that Kenny O'Donnell immediately played for the first eleven, thereby upsetting my rank order but they lived at some distance from the school and would not play for 1A in the class league, despite all my attempts at persuasion.

In September 1941 I broke new ground socially by attending my first wedding. It meant a day off school which was fine since it was not games day and the marriage was that of Aunt Julia and Uncle Joe, of whom we were very fond. They were both extremely good with children and had often baby-sat, or the 1930s equivalent of that word, when we were small. Uncle Joe could draw very well and had lived for some time in the United States. We loved his imitation of Schnozzle Durante whom he had actually seen in vaudeville and who was on our prescribed list of film stars. This was handed out impartially and at random by my mother. Joe E. Brown was also banned although I can't for the life of me think why. Anyway, we learned of Schnozzle's act second-hand and attended the wedding in good heart.

The ceremony was in St Margaret's Church, Kinning Park, just along the road from the *Ailsa Craig*, and the reception at the Georgic, in Union Street in the heart of town, which still had a mysterious attraction for us. My mother kept her promise that she would dance at her sister's wedding but only just. She was now severely crippled with arthritis and I cannot recollect that she ever danced again. I enjoyed the wedding but found it long, as I have always found weddings long. At 11 years old one was not of an age to mingle with the adults all the time but one was certainly beyond joining Philip and the young cousins in sliding up and down the highly polished floors of the reception suite. All our relatives sang all their particular songs and my mother bent a steely eye on us to prevent immoderate and misplaced laughter.

The highspot of the day was the evening visit to the Paramount Cinema — remember that we had never been to the "town pictures" — to see a film in which the latest sensation, Carmen Miranda, the Brazilian Bombshell, appeared with Don Ameche. There was a flood of Latin American films at this time and not by accident since Franklin Delano Roosevelt had let it be known that Hollywood should do its bit for the Good Neighbour policy by making pictures which showed South Americans in a good light. Our great joy was sadly alloyed when, with twenty minutes of the film remaining, the wretched Julie fell asleep and my mother decreed that we all had to go home. Furious, we stumbled along the passageway and up the aisles, leaving the intricacies of the plot of *Down Argentine Way* unresolved. Our darkest forebodings about girl children had been confirmed yet again. She had not been in the least sleepy while cavorting about the floor at the wedding, I remarked grimly to Frank.

The contradictions of life continued to strike us. My Aunt Julia, now married, resigned from teaching, as was the practice, at precisely the time that women conductresses began to appear on our tram cars. They were every bit as tough as the men and extremely capable. We were very impressed by one on the 12 route from Paisley Road Toll to Mount Florida. This lady spoke in a well-modulated voice like that of a BBC announcer, wore black leather gloves and invariably had a flower in the buttonhole of her uniform jacket. We always felt that we should pay more when we landed up on her tram.

At school I soon realised my good fortune in that my subjects fell into two clearly defined categories. They were either very good or very bad. English, History, Geography, the languages, Latin and French, and Music gave me no trouble whatsoever. My weakness lay on the Maths and Science side, although the full enormity of that weakness was as yet only hinted at. My Maths teacher, Anne Dawson, a buxom, handsome woman, spotted my inability to think mathematically at a time when it was still fairly successfully disguised by the arithmetical flair which I had inherited from my mother. Nor did Science appeal (there was then no distinction made between its various branches). I disliked the smell and lay-out of the labs and my natural ham-handedness made me tentative and apprehensive. It was tolerable in the initial stages because I liked the teacher we had. John Rogers was cool, leisurely, even languid. His nickname of "Sanny" was the most inappropriate of anyone of the staff. We got to know him well since he succeeded the maritime Mr Moffat as our form-master.

There were two sisters who took us irregularly for French and Latin. Their names were Betty and Mary Davidson but off-parade they were Lulu and Zulu and they provided a most interesting contrast in temperament. Betty (Lulu) was tall, thin, sallow and wore glasses. She had no difficulty at all in controlling a boy's class. Even Kenny O'Donnell who at less than 14 years of age was as near six feet as mattered not, was liable to receive a sidewinder to the ear and a muttered "It's the ABLATIVE UV IT, you goat!" We looked on aghast. Did this woman not realise that O'Donnell had made history by playing for the school first eleven in his first year? Her sister Zulu concentrated on French and was small, fluttery and easily reduced to tears. The handling of 43 boys is no light thing and we ranged from very young babyish lads to big fellows on the threshold of manhood.

As the nights drew in there was little else to do except homework; English and History were never a chore although I usually read the class home reader in at most two sittings and then sat for six months while the slower colleagues caught up. Our very first home reader was John Buchan's *Greenmantle*, an excellent choice for boys as was the same author's *Prester John* but it was asking a lot for the same age group to make much of *Silas Marner*.

It was during the dark nights, and after we had streaked our way through the home reader, that the district library came into its own. We had two local libraries, Langside Library which was at the foot of the Monument Hill on the Battlefield side, and the Campbell Library in Pollokshaws, a strange structure to which the entry lay through a wide pend. Langside was our clear favourite and there we used to go clutching the heavy paste-board tickets which bore differing colours for fiction and non-fiction. We were still rigidly confined to the Children's Section although I kept chipping away at the head librarian in the hope of a premature promotion.

There were some odd books in the Children's Section — the *Rise and Fall of the Dutch Republic* was certainly one — and there were any God's amount of G A Henty novels. George Alfred Henty specialised in books bearing such titles as *With Clive in India, With Lee in Virginia, With Wolfe at Quebec* and so on. Had he still been around he would have been busy writing *With Montgomery at Alamein.* His books were identikit, with clever, young, clean-cut heroes who came to the notice of king, emperor, general, by reason of deeds of bravery and coolness in battle. Pluck was a word much esteemed by George Alfred. I see clearly now that he must simply have looked up biographies of the great men in question and then basically written the same story, changing only names and locale. Still, his books had an undeniable vigour about them and I much preferred them to the Biggles stories or the dreadful *Children's History* of Arthur Mee which must have sickened many a potential historian. There were enough Henty books and *Just William* stories to keep a fellow going for a very long time.

We had books at home, of course, not many but a few interesting ones among them, notably a Western whose title, *The Red Rider of Smoky Range* remains in my mind although the authorship does not. It may have been written by W C Tuttle who, with Zane Grey, was a Western writer of repute at the time. There were a couple of early Wodehouses, notably *Leave it to Psmith* which for the first time provided me with the experience of laughing out loud while reading. There was a *History of Ireland* by the exotically named D'Arcy McGhee and, rather more improbably, *The Way of All Flesh* by Samuel Butler. I read my way methodically along our meagre shelves.

We did not always read such exalted literature of course. We had, at least Frank and I had, by great good fortune graduated from the *Rainbow* and *Chick's Own* to those stirring papers for boys, the *Hotspur*, the *Adventure*, the *Rover*, the *Wizard* and the *Skipper*. These were our weekly purchases, although I suppose in strict accuracy we bought the *Hotspur* and the *Adventure* and swopped for the rest. The stories were well written and astonishingly informative. Many of them involved mythical public schools and I am certain that Red Circle School in the *Hotspur* was far better known in Scotland than the over-praised Greyfriars. A great favourite in the *Adventure* was "Red Fergie", the story not of a Pollokshaws youth but of a Jacobite agent who tied down an army of Redcoats in the Highlands after Culloden. It was a shameless lift from *Kidnapped* although years passed before I realised this. There was science fiction even in those days. In the *Hotspur*, during the first winter of the war, there was a story called "Last Rocket to Venus" which dealt with the question of who should be saved from an earth which was freezing to extinction. It was a rather clever variation on the balloon game and who should be pitched out.

There were sagas of the football field, one bore the riveting title "A Hundred goals for Slasher Kane — or Death!" Slasher Kane was a centre-forward who was being threatened by A Gang with fate unspeakable if he did not score 100 goals in a season, about twice the going rate of even the most legendary Dixie Dean/Jimmy McGrory centres. Not wishing to encounter this fate, Slasher was naturally in the market to take all free kicks and penalties, frequently elbowing his colleagues aside to do so, thus causing severe comments from the terracing on his selfishness as the supporters knew nothing of the strain under which poor Slasher laboured.

At the other end of the field in another yarn, the deeds of "Cast Iron Bill" came under scrutiny. He was a goalkeeper who in all his long career in League football had never conceded a single goal. Occasionally all seemed lost and on at least two occasions an instalment ended with Bill helpless on his back and the ball sailing towards an empty net. But thanks in the first instance to a sudden Force Eight gale which blew the ball outside the posts and in the second to a passing sniper in the crowd who shot the ball (although it was never made clear just why the itinerant marksman should have been there) Bill's charge was preserved intact, as the writer could never resist saying.

Gradually stories came to reflect the war and Dixie Dale, the popular sports master of Red Circle was called away on Secret Service work and great was the sorrow when he was duly killed off some weeks later. Then we began to notice a mysterious tramp hanging around the gates of Red Circle, wishing to speak to the School Captain most particularly. Could this possibly be . . . ? It was.

When I had been tipped by aunts or visitors, my most fruitful sources, I would sometimes buy the paperbacks which narrated the cases of the detectives, Sexton Blake, and the more interesting Dixon Hawke. At fourpence these were excellent value and intelligently written, although riddled with class prejudice and dislike of foreigners. Hawke's assistant was a cheerful youth of faintly East End provenance called Tommy Burke who always addressed the great man as "Guv'nor". Their major adversary was a beautiful Spanish noblewoman who among other useful attributes could adopt a cataleptic state at will. More than one case ended with Hawke saying ruminatively, "I have a feeling that we have not seen the last of the beautiful Countess X." No more we had. I was genuinely sad when the wartime shortage of paper killed off Hawke for good in this medium.

Rather than be without reading material, always a risk if you read as quickly as I did, I purloined my mother's magazine, the famous womens' weekly paper the *People's Friend*. It had on an average week three serials and two complete stories and could scarcely have been further removed from real Scottish life in the 1940s. The authors had names like Lesley Farquhar or Ishbel (never Isobel) McGregor and the stories were about a family in Dumbreck or another of the better-class districts in Glasgow or some couthy kailyard small Scots town. The women were of impregnable virtue, even I could see that. The most unsympathetic of the young females was never portrayed as anything worse than calculating and flinty-hearted. The heroes were dependable and quiet, and in character shot glints of quiet amusement from their eyes. A favourite story-line had the girl deciding to leave her native village of Auchmithie for the junketing of Glasgow or London. With an ache in his heart, the handsome young minister who was very often called Keith or Ninian, would acquiesce in the lass's decision to leave home.

"London's the place for a girl like you," he would say manfully
through misty eyes. I thought that this was such a fine line that I was
overjoyed when Joan Buchan, my first girlfriend, left Holy Cross to
go to the capital. I delightedly seized the chance to use this magical
phrase, "London's the place for a girl like you". I delivered it
beautifully and I can still see the look of sheer bafflement on her
seven-year-old face.

In the *People's Friend* of course the heroine (unlike Joan whom I
never saw again) soon repented of her mad hankering for gaiety and
returned to Auchmithie and quiet, handsome, glinting Keith or
Ninian. If by some odd chance there was no handsome young
minister in the story there was certain to be a wise, kindly older one
very often called Ninian or Keith. The *People's Friend* took
absolutely no notice of the hundreds of thousands of Catholics,
Episcopalians, Jews and Nonconformists who dwelt in Scotland
even then. I glanced at one the other day and almost nothing had
changed. For a certain type of Scotswoman it was a splendid
anodyne. I formed a powerful ambition to get a letter of mine
published in it and receive the much-coveted prize of a tea-caddy.

Phil meanwhile was still on a literary diet of *Tiny Tots* although he
had been promised that if he worked hard at his reading he might be
promoted to *Playbox*. His present reading-matter, *Tiny Tots*, dealt
in hyphenated words and the main character on the front page was
Nursie. It was a very gentle, middle-class, essentially Home
Counties paper which every week contained a letter from the Editor
which always began with the same address

> To my little friend where'er you may be
> In Great Britain or over the sea.

Even before the war such papers were coming under fire from the
more rumbustious publications such as the *Dandy* and *Beano*. They
were not looked on with any great favour by my mother and such
comics as *Chips* and *Jingles*, printed on *coloured paper* for heaven's
sake, were beyond consideration. Even with this ban we were not
short of things to read and the ability to read and the enjoyment of
reading were godsends in the long winter nights when so many other
doors were literally closed to us.

Homework done and, very importantly, seen to be done, we
could listen to the radio. By late 1941 we were just beginning to
mount regular bombing raids in some strength on Europe and right
from the beginning I identified with the bomber pilots in a way that I

had not quite been able to do with their fighter colleagues of 1940, although profoundly grateful to them, like everyone else. I think that what most impressed me about bomber crews was their requirement to endure great hardships passively. A fighter pilot to a large extent controlled his own destiny and was operating in very short furious bursts, these fellows were not. They were the long-distance runners to Fighter Command's sprinters. In unheated, unpressurised planes they were making flights which grew longer as the war progressed — before too long they would be attacking Northern Italy. They had to contend with attacks from night fighters and anti-aircraft batteries and weather which could have changed dramatically in the six hours or more that they had been away. It was not difficult to picture the isolation of the rear gunner in his aft turret, nor to figure out his chances of clearing the plane should it be hit. At least the pilot, co-pilot and navigator were constantly employed during the flight. They were brave men, as indeed were the Germans who from time to time made the night dangerous and uncomfortable.

Britain was now a nation of large factories and the radio programmes took account of this with offerings such as *Music While You Work*, essentially anodyne and harmless, *Workers' Playtime* and *Works Wonders*. These last were differentiated by their casts. *Workers' Playtimes* were conventional variety shows with well-known names who varied their acts by references to Big Alf the foreman, thereby guaranteeing themselves a laugh on the spot while anaesthetising listeners who neither knew of nor cared for the in-house joke. *Works Wonders* was quite another matter. This was essentially a "Go As You Please" series with the entertainment provided by members of the labour force itself. There was the very occasional jewel among the dross but there was tons of dross. Laryngeal tenors croaked out *The English Rose*, Fred from the turning shop did ungifted impersonations and the works band assaulted *There'll Always Be an England*. Always the works band played special arrangements, credited to their bandmaster and without exception these showed the advisability of leaving such to trained professional musicians. The value of such programmes of course was not in the standards attained — many of them should, bluntly, never have been inflicted on paying licence-holders — but in the psychological boost which hearing one's name conferred and the fact that the work of a factory was being recognised, even if disguised as "somewhere in the West Country".

Then, at last, the Americans were in. I was staying with my grandmother over a weekend when the news came through. Churchill's
reaction was immediate. He knew that now the Allies would win.
The radio was quick to urge caution, there could be no American
troops here for many months, and one far-seeing commentator
pointed out that for the Americans, the Pacific might prove to be the
more important theatre of operations. There was however great
rejoicing. We didn't rate the Japanese highly, for we knew that
Singapore was impregnable and that the British presence was loved
throughout the Far East. As *The Russian Rose* had done six months
or so before, *Over There* suddenly burst upon the air waves.

In our own little sphere we were even more excited by the thought
that we were going to England for a holiday. After their wedding,
Uncle Joe had been assigned to war work in Manchester and Aunt
Julia had gone with him. To our great delight they invited us down
over the Christmas holidays and after some coaxing our parents
agreed to let us go. We were leaping about with anticipation and I
gave the other two the benefit of my previous travelling experience
in England, having gone in 1937 to Newcastle on a one-day Sunday
excursion with my grandmother. We were in ecstasies as we
travelled south unaccompanied in the unheated, gloomy train
which had no refreshment-car facilities whatsoever.

Undeterred, we pulled out our flasks and offered our sandwiches
to our fellow-travellers. To our relief and delight, this kind offer was
refused and we proceeded to demolish the food. We tried to work
out where we were although this was difficult since the names of all
railway stations had been removed in 1940 to confuse the invading
Germans. They did not come over to be confused but the great
British public were assuredly baffled as the only identification on
rail journeys was an invariable gabble in the local *patois* by a porter
from a darkened station platform. The craze for anonymity reached
astonishing heights with firms such as the Richmond Park Laundry
Company being required to remove the offending first two words
from their fleet of vans although had the Germans got that far, the
well-meant subterfuge would scarcely have detained them.

On our arrival at Manchester we were met at the station only by
my Aunt Julia. Uncle Joe had been moved at very short notice to
help with a rush job at Maryport in Cumberland. This was a great
disappointment for us and an unlooked-for burden for my young
aunt but she coped admirably. It meant no football, since it was
decided that we couldn't go to a match in case there was an air-raid,

and the sirens went on each of the six nights that we were there. The chance of seeing Stockport County therefore fell by the wayside but we busied ourselves happily in other directions. We went into the centre of Manchester and saw for ourselves what real bomb damage was like. We had not visited Clydebank.

The house where my aunt was lodging was in the Heaton Moor district and we wandered around there happily, paying several visits to the cinema in company with Hilary, the daughter of the house and of an age with myself. One film stood out, *The Mark of Zorro*. We thought it was wonderful and we particularly liked the moment when the dandified Tyrone Power, returned from Spain, asked Eugene Palette who was playing the crusty but patriotic friar if he would like to see some sleight-of-hand tricks. Tyrone was sound enough and patriotic too, for was he himself not the noted Zorro? He was. He wreaked enormous damage on the royal forces who were quite unable to run him to earth. One exchange lingers when a sentry on finding a dead colleague calls this to the attention of the guard commander who makes an instant diagnosis:

> "Zorro did this!"
> "How do you know it's Zorro, sir?"
> "He's (the corpse) got a zee on his chest."

So Zorro dodged the royalist forces, we dodged the bombs and I courted Hilary. She had let me hold her hand under cover of darkness in the cinema but love died next day when she thrashed me comprehensively at table tennis and offered the opinion that I wasn't really very good, was I? We packed, thanked my aunt sincerely, caught the train, politely offered sandwiches, knew where we were this time and returned to give our war correspondent experience to family and friends in the more peaceful north.

Chapter Five

1942:
The end of the beginning

I remember 1942 as the year in which we stopped looking back to pre-war days. From now on our talk was mostly about what life would be like when it, the war, was all over.

My father was gradually regaining fitness, aided by a very restricted diet which demanded that he subsist exclusively on fish, tripe and eggs. Fish and tripe were unrationed and he had a special ration book which entitled him to extra eggs and milk. He continued to run the pub on his own and fight his way home at night through the black-out on crowded, darkened tramcars. At least he had an earlier closure now than in peacetime, at nine o'clock, although that in itself was a direct result of the crippling shortage of supplies.

On occasional visits which I made to the *Ailsa Craig* my father would indicate the various beer crates — Younger's, Fowler's, McEwan's, Steel Coulson's, Murrays . . . there were many more brewers then than now — and tell me how allocations were being cut. If beer was difficult, whisky was impossible. His monthly quota from one of the big distillers such as Bell's, Crawford's or Haig's would be six bottles at best. The claims of regular customers had to be balanced against those of servicemen on leave, for no shortage was more grudgingly borne by the civilian population than that of whisky. The difficulty was compounded by the fact that a pub's allocation was based on its pre-war turnover. As my father had only bought the *Ailsa Craig* in 1938, at the time of the great Empire Exhibition, he was still in the process of building up the business at the outbreak of war and his entitlement was therefore small.

He had borrowed from the brewers to set himself up and my mother, with the strict financial principles of her generation and perhaps a memory of old Tam Todd, her former employer at Todd, Cunningham, Petrie, a prominent firm of Glasgow warehouse-men, insisted that the loan be paid off as quickly as possible. My father doubted the wisdom of this, feeling that as long as he was the brewer's debtor, there would be a vested interest in supplying him, but he allowed himself to be persuaded. His misgivings were in the long run well founded, although in general my mother had the more acute business brain. She kept the books in order and I occasionally helped her. My father could certainly have used some help in the pub, even if only for the bottling of empties in the cellar. While this would have been illegal for me at the age of 13, I should have tried to break the law more often, particularly since I flouted it in aspects which were far less useful. The running of a one-man pub was an onerous, unremitting treadmill, how much so can be seen by the fact that the wartime closures on Thursday evenings and the facility for taking a fortnight's summer holiday were seen as radical advances in conditions. Before the war, the only holiday guaranteed to a Scottish publican was that of New Year's Day.

In the spring of 1942 the war came as physically near to us as it was ever to get. We stayed at 207 Deanston Drive and a tenement at the other end of the street, somewhere in the 20s, was completely destroyed by a direct hit from a land-mine. The air-raid shelter in the back-green was completely obliterated and the death toll was heavy—18 or so. Fortunately for us, Deanston Drive was a long street, almost half a mile in length, and we were certainly some 500 yards away. Even so, the noise in our own shelter was of a volume which dazed us and several windows in adjacent houses were cracked by the blast.

The news of the bombing got around very quickly the next morning in the mysterious way that all wartime news, real and imagined, did and Frank, Phil and I ran along the street to see for ourselves. Beyond Skirving Street the Drive was barricaded off and we were very rightly told to get to hell out of it by a weary, begrimed ARP warden. We went but not before we had seen the stretcher-bearers trying to keep their balance as they slithered over the rubble with their sheeted dead.

The spring bombing of Deanston Drive served to dispel a South Glasgow myth which had been quietly but sedulously spread in the first years of the war. This was that Shawlands was the safest district in Glasgow and would never be bombed by the Luftwaffe because Hitler's sister lived there. I made great sport with this notion and in so doing gave much pain to my grandmother who thought that I was being nastily cynical. I suggested that it was very possible that Hitler did not like his sister and that this would render Shawlands a particularly unsafe place to be. I invented various Christian names for this mysterious lady, of which Bridget Hitler was my favourite. I expressed surprise that, having consulted the telephone directory, she did not appear to be listed although I was perfectly prepared to concede that she might be Bridget McClintock or, better, Bridget Morgenstern.

While I exercised my wit over the raid the effect on my young brother Phil was much more direct. He had appeared unperturbed in the shelter during the raid — we were all in fact unnaturally calm — but when the bombers arrived Philip had received prior warning. With Frank, he attended St Conval's School in Pollokshaws and his teacher was the celebrated Wiggy Campbell, a lady whose hairstyle was formidable but ultimately unconvincing. Her class on the day of the raid had behaved even more abominably than usual and since in that class Philip was regarded as a model of deportment the real larrikins must have been noteworthy. The poor, exasperated woman, when prayers had been reached at the end of the day, informed the class that they had been very badly behaved girls and boys and that God would undoubtedly send the German bombers that night to punish them. In this she was merely speaking with the Old Testament fervour of a Catholic primary teacher of the time but the Luftwaffe arrived as per contract, with the results which have been described. To a boy, or girl, Phil's class was convinced that Wiggy Campbell was a German spy and for the next four weeks the unfortunate woman was dogged by a posse of P4 pupils, anxious to catch her in the act of passing information.

The possible passing of information to hostile sources was something which obsessed the Government. There were constant campaigns on the themes of "Walls Have Ears" and "Careless Talk Costs Lives". There was one Government poster which caused great offence even at the height of a world war. "Be like dad. Keep mum!" may have sounded fine in a copy-writer's office but it drew protests from almost every women's organisation even in a non-feminist age.

The cinema too was replete with short Ministry of Information films on the subject of "Careless Talk". A fairly standard plot would show a rash young subaltern who while dining with his girlfriend in a West End restaurant would roar to her at the pitch of his voice Allied plans and dispositions for a forthcoming landing. The waiter, so hovering, foreign and villainous-looking that a man of normal prudence would have refrained from discussing the weather in his presence, was later seen transmitting his newly gleaned knowledge to the Fatherland. The outcome was the failure of the raid or expedition, the sustaining of heavy Allied casualties and the film ending with the minatory words, "Careless Talk Costs Lives".

In the early days of the war, cinemas had had to be cleared when the sirens sounded, although such soundings then were almost always false alarms. Later on, it was usual for a notice to be flashed on the screen to the effect that an air-raid was in progress but that the performance would continue. When visiting one of the three Shawlands cinemas, the Embassy, Elephant or Waverley in receding order of distance from our house, we were under strict instructions to come home the moment this notice hit the screen. One Saturday afternoon, therefore, we left, with much muttering, Robert Donat as Sir Thomas Culpepper to the vengeance of Charles Laughton as Henry VIII. Scarcely had we set foot in the house when the all-clear sounded. We returned in haste to the Embassy where ten minutes' negotiation with the doorman successfully reinstated us.

By this time I was once more in employment, delivering papers for Barr's, the newsagents in Kilmarnock Road. I was fully a year short of the legal age for performing this work and incredibly in 1942 such things still mattered. I had to hide in the back shop or rush out if there was a pending visit from the inspectors. The pay for delivering evening newspapers was tenpence per night and one of the advantages of working for Barr's was that they did not deliver on Saturdays, thus leaving that afternoon free for match-going. Morning deliveries brought in seven shillings and sixpence weekly, but it was a cold business trudging through the unlighted winter streets or, huddling under the glimmer of a stairhead lamp, trying to beat my customers to the news.

In the early months of 1942 that news was being made by the Japanese. At the time of Japan's entry into the war there was a very brief attempt to represent the Japanese as comic turns, to cast them in the roles that the Italians occupied almost throughout the conflict. They were undersized, short-sighted imitators, nothing more. That attitude soon changed—*very soon* changed. Hong Kong was to hold and it didn't. Singapore was impregnable and it wasn't. *Repulse* and *Prince of Wales* were unsinkable and they were sunk. At once the organs of propaganda altered course by 180 degrees. The qualities of woodcraft and ferocity that marked the American Indian were transferred to the Japanese soldier. So too was the gulf that separated him from European standards of civilisation.

I remember reading while on my paper round one evening in the January of 1942 a speech Anthony Eden made as Foreign Secretary. Referring in the House to the fall of Hong Kong, he said that wounded British soldiers had been bayoneted to death, civilians shot and nurses raped and murdered. The account went on, "At every statement little gasps of horror came from the House." I had no clear idea of what rape was, except that it was something which happened only to women and was very bad. In a film of the time, Claudette Colbert, trapped before the Japanese advance in the Phillippines, gasped out that the American men would be killed "and the women . . .". She left the rest unsaid.

With the entry of Japan into the war, things got harder on the home front, immediately and noticeably. Oil became scarcer and so increasingly did rubber. It was the end of what little pleasure motoring remained and frenzied attempts were made to find a substitute for petrol. Certain bus routes, including the 4A which linked us to our spiritual home in Mount Florida, went over to gas-trailer buses. These found great difficulty in negotiating the hill at Battlefield Monument and, ever willing to assist the war effort, we used to jump from the bus at the foot of the hill, steam past an embarrassed driver and rejoin the vehicle at the summit. I can't believe that the 18 stone in total which we took from the bus made all that difference but we felt very magnanimous.

Philip in fact never travelled down the Monument Hill either, being convinced that the bus was going to overturn on the sharp bend halfway down the brae. He used to skip nimbly off the bus at Shand's Funeral Offices at the top of the hill and still had sufficient reserves of pace to arrive at the foot comfortably before the sluggish gas-propelled bus.

The tyres for our bikes and our tennis balls and footballs went up in the palls of smoke that shrouded the Malayan and Burmese towns. Our diet dwindled in variety. We bade a reluctant farewell to the pineapple chunks and mandarin oranges which had brightened breakfast. The Ministry of Food redoubled its efforts to tell us that we were better off without such inessential fripperies. The strong possibility that this might very well be true did not make their propaganda any less irksome.

Once the black-out had been safely negotiated, Glasgow had a thriving night life. We were far too young to go to the dancing of course (dancing in Glasgow was always preceded by the definite article) and had to rely on older female cousins for tales of the Americans, not greatly in evidence as yet. Nor were we allowed to go on our own to the "town pictures" which meant anywhere nearer the city centre than Eglinton Toll.

Each Christmas however, we did the rounds of the pantomimes, never seeing less than two and sometimes as many as four. The Glasgow pantomime was an astonishing institution and unlike its anaemic counterpart in the south, a good Glasgow pantomime would still be going strong in mid-March and indeed some only closed with the Easter holidays. During the war, the Alhambra usually had Will Fyffe and Harry Gordon as top of the bill. Gordon, an Aberdonian, played the Dame and seized the chance of war to enlarge his repertoire with such songs as *I'm one of the oldest hens in the Wrens* (the WRNS or Women's Royal Naval Service was like its sister organisations, the Auxiliary Territorial Service and the Women's Auxiliary Air Force, good for a usually affectionate laugh). Will Fyffe specialised in pawky, philosophical shipyard workers, cutty pipe in hand. His great song was *Clyde Built* which ended

> Ay, she's Clyde-built and of a' the ships afloat
> Ye'll never find a better than a Clyde-built boat.

He was always guaranteed a huge hand when after musing on the sorrows of war he would break off and say, "Aye, well . . . mebbe next year".

I preferred Jack Anthony at the Pavilion with his smooth straight man, Bond Rowell, whom a daring pal of ours called Round Bowel. Topical allusion was Anthony's forte and he would improvise — or appear to improvise — couplets on the names of Scottish regiments or divisions. Thus, in the pantomime of Christmas 1942 in the immediate wake of El Alamein and having asked the audience for the name of a fighting body, someone in the stalls, almost certainly a "plant", called out, "The 51st Division", a very popular Highland unit. Jack Anthony appeared to think for a few seconds before rattling out:

> Out in the desert the heat's terrific
> And the dust obscures your vision,
> It's only the dust of Rommel's troops
> Being chased by the 51st Division.

A regular in wartime Pavilion pantomimes was G H Elliott, billed then, which he certainly would not be now, as The Chocolate-Coloured Coon. I found his act, which consisted of minstrel songs sung in a high falsetto to the accompaniment of indifferent soft-shoe dancing, tedious in the extreme but the interest lay in the subterfuges by which the plantation minstrel could be introduced to such frolics as *Aladdin*.

At the Royal the star was Dave Willis who concentrated his attention on the home front in such songs as *The Barrage Balloon Blower-Upper*:

> I'm a barrage-balloon blower-upper,
> I blow up the barrage balloons
> Oh it's no wonder that I get the hump,
> I blow them all up with my bicycle pump.

His other song, *The nicest-looking warden in the ARP* won him national celebrity with its Duke of Plaza Toro realism in the event of an air raid.

> Ah'll jump in my shelter but don't you follow me,
> There's no room in ma shelter for it's far too wee.

Away from the war Willis could be extremely droll and I cherished and sang for months afterwards his Alpine guide song:

> Ah am a Tyrolean,
> No' a big yin, just a wee yin,
> Ah climb the rocky mountains,
> Away up a 'ky.

This last line was Willis's trademark or catchphrase, to use the term increasingly coming into vogue, nowhere more so than on radio. Radio was king in those wartime years and while chief interest inevitably centred on the news bulletins, variety shows had their massive and loyal audiences. The programme which attracted the largest number of listeners was ITMA *(It's That Man Again)* with Tommy Handley in the title role. The script was fairly feeble but various memorable characters emerged, such as Funf the German spy and the bibulous Colonel Chinstrap. The complaining char, Mona Lott and the over-efficient secretary, Miss Hotchkiss, were typical of the characters who were dragged in merely to say their tag lines—in Mona Lott's case, "It's being so cheerful as keeps me going".

Happidrome was a traditional north-country music hall programme which gained national as opposed to regional exposure about this time. Harry Korris was the jovial MC, Mr Lovejoy, and he was assisted by the gormless Enoch and the Establishment man, Ramsbottom. A highlight of the weekly bill was the tap-dancing of Enoch, an odd item for a radio show one might think but no odder than the ventriloquist act which was the mainspring of Edgar Bergen and Charlie McCarthy, an American programme soon to burst on us. Established music-hall acts such as Rawicz and Landauer, the Polish pianists, Billy Russell the comedian, vocalists Bob and Alf Pearson and the impressionist Florence Desmond all appeared on *Happidrome* but the introduction of the very first American programmes for their troops in Europe served to show how homespun the British comedy product was.

Comedians such as Bob Hope, Jack Benny and, most gifted of all, Fred Allen, showed that there could be such a thing as situation comedy with credible and interesting characters. The most distinguished, if not necessarily the best, American programmes were those with a high guest appearance content such as *Command Performance* and *Mail Call*. These came on comparatively late in the evening and the rule of our house was that they could be heard "if ready for bed". It was, therefore, in pyjamas and dressing-gown, clutching a cup of watery cocoa, that we heard Harry James play trumpet, Eddie Cantor sing, and Charles Laughton give the Gettysburg Address. Even as a young boy, it was clear to me that the British worshipped reticence and reserve while the Americans did not. The Yanks sang the *Battle Hymn of the Republic* with a simple and simplistic fervour whereas the British tended towards acute embarrassment when it became necessary to sing *Land of Hope and Glory*. American tunes were now beginning to dominate the air waves, especially the bouncy *Don't sit under the apple tree with anyone else but me* and *Deep in the heart of Texas*, a truly dire song which by virtue of incessant playing attained eventually a wide popularity. There was a great emphasis placed on the faithfulness of the girls who stayed behind with titles such as *I don't want to walk without you, baby*, and later *No love, no nothing, no not until my baby comes home.* We didn't know about the Dear John letters that were flying about in abundance and would not have understood them if we had.

Towards the end of 1942 we had a chance to see the Americans at first hand. On a Saturday afternoon in October the American forces took over Hampden Park for the day to give an exhibition of baseball and softball. We were not enchanted by the news and would much have preferred to have watched our beloved Queen's Park but curiosity drew us along. The athletic side of the venture was only moderately successful if for no other reason than that the football pitch was entirely the wrong shape for baseball, but much interest was created by the presence on the ground of the American film star Edward G Robinson. He seized the chance to address the crowd, or rather he was there for that very purpose and told us that compared to Hitler, his (Edward G's) gangsters were cissies. "But we are not going to allow this gangster to take democracy for a ride, as my gangster boys used to say." The contrast was all the more pointed when he was followed to the microphone by the Foreign Secretary Anthony Eden who murmured a few platitudes in received English and then retired with his curiously engaging smile and toss of the head.

This was the point of the war which could fairly be described as the end of the beginning. The country was moving away from the largely passive role which it had sustained for the first three years. Air-raids on Germany became heavier and more frequent while London had some respite from the incessant nightly battering. There were still isolated raids on Glasgow and in one of them a handsome Greek Thomson church was destroyed in Langside Road within half a mile of the school, but air-raids had ceased to figure largely in our lives.

In August, to our high delight, we had gone back to Kirn. The black-out never seemed so oppressive there. There were always pin-pricks of light from careless ships on the Firth and in any event Double Summer Time meant that in our northern latitudes it was light until ten o'clock in the evening, even in August. One source of light was now missing from the river, though, for the neutral ships had all but gone. The Norwegian, Dutch and Danish vessels which had literally stood out in 1940 were all now in enemy hands or in the drab grey uniform of the Allied merchant fleet. We badly missed the colourful liveries of the pre-war Clyde steamers and were always hopeful that the war would be resolved with a sudden master-stroke. Two events in the course of this holiday falsely raised our expectations.

We had just newly arrived and been sent into Dunoon to get temporary ration cards at the Food Office there, always the first task of a wartime holiday. This errand accomplished, we then registered with McDougall's, the largest grocers in Kirn, and after tea went down to the coal pier as we always did. To our great excitement an unknown paddle steamer was making its way over from Kilcreggan. We were all absolute experts on Clyde steamers and knew that the ship was not the *Queen Mary II*, not that this called for any great expertise since the *Queen Mary II* was a turbine steamer. But this mystery ship was not the *Marchioness of Lorne* either, which was a paddler certainly but one of the new concealed paddle-box atrocities and although our nickname for the *Marchioness*, "Stumpy", was affectionate enough, it indicated that her lines were not things of beauty. The *Lucy Ashton* was beautiful but this paddler was not the *Lucy Ashton* and the three boats already named were the only ones which served the upper Clyde piers during those war years. So, what on earth was this steamer?

As the eldest brother, and drawing on my longer pre-war memories, I thought that it might be the *Glen Rosa* or the *Queen Empress*. I would have said the *Marmion* perhaps, for the newcomer looked like an LNER boat but I knew that the *Marmion* had been sunk the year before while minesweeping off Harwich. My guess that the boat had come from Craigendoran, the pier from which the LNER steamers operated, was in fact a good one for the paddle steamer was a former North British boat and the North British had been the forerunner of the LNER. The mystery boat was the *Fair Maid* which pre-war had been an excursion steamer on the Firth of Forth. Her arrival at Kirn on that still, August evening of 1942 had nothing to do with a sudden end to the war but was merely the completion of a nightly voyage which brought war workers from the naval and seaplane bases in the Gare Loch and Loch Long.

There was also a strange little coaster, the St Mawes, from a Cornish port which ferried munitions workers over from Greenock and which tied up to the coal pier in the still, late evenings. We much admired the practised skill with which the workers leapt ashore almost before the gangway was down.

A few days later we were certain that things were moving fast as the newspaper headlines screamed "Landing in France". We broke off our afternoon spell of "Three and In"—a restricted form of football played by us three brothers in which the scorer of three goals was penalised by having to take a turn in goal—to ask a passing, elderly man, "Is this the invasion, mister?"

He looked at us with faint annoyance and grunted, "Well, we're in and they'll have to get us out."

We dashed back to our house in Kirn Brae but as we had no radio in our holiday home we were forced to contain ourselves until the

next morning's papers arrived with news of Dieppe. It was at once
evident that the British Government had stopped just short of telling the French people that this was an army of liberation and within
a day or so the phrases "phased withdrawal" and "objectives
achieved" which we had come to associate unswervingly with
defeat, were freely sprinkled across the communiqués.

News readers had lost their anonymity at the time of the
threatened German invasion in 1940 when they were allowed to
reveal their identify to give added credence to the bulletins. The
announcers became very famous. Names such as Frank Phillips,
Stewart Hibbert, Alvar Liddell and Joseph McLeod were literally
household names. We had our favourite among them. Alvar Liddell
was always associated with cheerful, upbeat news while Joseph
McLeod, whose voice seemed to have a more melancholy tinge, was
linked, no doubt quite unjustly, with calamity—after the war the listening public was allowed to learn that Alvar Liddell had a very pleasant
voice and his rendition of *I'll Walk Beside You* became a constant in
record programmes.

In the long-term the Dieppe raid had its uses but its immediate
impact was doom-laden enough. We had no relatives in the
American or Australian forces and we were perhaps rather unusual
in this. Our sole contact in the overseas services was a Canadian
cousin who was serving with the Princess Patricia's Light Infantry.
By chance he came on leave to us a few weeks after we returned from
the coast and he was quietly vehement in his denunciation of the
handling of the Dieppe affair. We were particularly astonished at
his charge, made with great passion and sincerity, that the generals
had been less tender of Canadian lives than they would have been of
British. Right or wrong he may have been, but one thing was certain.
Dieppe was not the long awaited invasion and another winter was in
immediate prospect with its relentless darkness. Our reluctance to
see the end of Double Summer Time was emphatically not shared by
the farmers who cordially loathed it. My father, with his country-
man's background, muttered that well they might since it entailed
rising at four in the morning sun time or, as he called it, God's time,
to look after livestock.

Going back to school was something to look forward to, all in all.
Our 43 boys of Class 1A had been reduced to 27 of 2A and although
the academic level may have been raised, we had lost virtually every
good footballer in the class. Still, I liked my new French teacher,
Cissie Foxworthy, who was very French-looking in what I later

came to realise was a Francoise Rosay/Simone Signoret way. She had a commendably relaxed attitude towards her classes and if for the first 40 minutes of a double period we worked hard, she would give us five minutes off to watch the classes playing football on the playing fields which were directly outside the classroom window. She would also play Jean Sablon and Tino Rossi records, and I would warble throatily *La Chanson des rues*, *Le bateau des îles*, and of course *J'attendrai*. Cissie's success was the more impressive in that she was following a hard act, the darkly handsome Johnny O'Hagan who had first introduced us to the language but who was now with the Forces.

Johnny had taught us a lullaby which he had picked up from Breton sailors on a French destroyer which had visited the Clyde a month before the war began. I remember the gently-bobbing tune and the words:

> Ici nous allons en bateau
> Par un ciel bleu, par un temps clair
> La mer vaut la campagne.

My brother Frank had now joined me at Holyrood, very bright but very young also. He had only just turned ten when he made the transition from primary to secondary school. I showed him the ropes and showed off dreadfully while doing so. He was giving away almost two years to his classmates, some of whom could almost have passed as his young uncles.

There was a bustle about a wartime school. We were constantly being exhorted to save waste paper, to collect old books and ledgers, to throw nothing out. Waste-paper sacks hung in every close and ranks were awarded according to how much paper one brought into school. Phil, a tireless collector, or purloiner of other people's paper, was rewarded with the rank of Air Vice-Marshal, a dignity from the heights of which he could more closely scrutinise the doings of Wiggy Campbell.

People fell in line with the most lunatic schemes of government. There was a remarkable civilian docility. The disasters in the Far East had convinced the Australians, and eventually ourselves, that we were not taking the war sufficiently seriously. The country therefore punished itself in a bizarre variety of ways. Lord Beaverbrook, when Minister for Aircraft Production, had insisted that parks, private houses and schools should lose their ornamental railings, which were to be melted down to make metal for aeroplanes. So too were the saucepans of those housewives who trustingly answered the call for them. Now, as Minister of War Production, Beaverbrook really cut loose and this at a time when, contrary to legend, Germany was further from total war than we were and domestic service, which had all but disappeared in Britain, was still a commonplace of life in the Third Reich. When we had collected papers until wearied of it, there was then a drive for rose hips, seen as an important source of Vitamin C. Mount Florida was still sufficiently rustic to have hedgerows conveniently to hand and we went out prospecting, though our hearts were not in it.

Equally half-hearted was our response to the "Dig for Victory" campaign. We scratched a patch of earth in the back-green, strewed a packet of seeds over it (we didn't like lettuce much and our grandmother had to nag us quite a bit to make us go to Woolworth's at Shawlands Cross where we bought the seeds) and then went away. When a few timid leaves appeared we ate them on sight and when nothing further happened we blamed the soil rather than our lack of husbandry. Somehow, against all the odds and from total ignorance, Philip managed to grow a perfectly respectable turnip. We debated eagerly the circumstances under which we would eat this exquisite vegetable and with what accompaniments but on going to bear it kitchenwards in triumph we discovered that some neighbour, jealous of our market gardening skills, had acquired our turnip. We gave up.

Above all in 1942, we stood in queues. Shawlands queues consisted of middle-aged women, dutiful wee girls and the Crampsey boys. We didn't mind queueing much, except on Saturday mornings when it badly affected our football, but clearly our mother was not physically capable of standing in queues for hours and in the queues there was often an invigorating conspiratorial cheerfulness. The rationed foods were easy, the trick was to know when the unrationed but scarce commodities, sweets, liver, chocolate biscuits, would be coming in.

Queues often formed on the merest whim or breath of rumour and where coupons had to be clipped or cancelled, serving took an eternity. There were Saturday mornings in the City Bakeries queue in Regwood Street where all life came down to getting half a dozen cream (artificial) cookies. Initially we made ill-advised attempts to get 18 cream (artificial) cookies but this was thwarted by indignant shouts of "Those three are brothers!" and, indeed, there was no denying it physically. Hamlet's mother was reputed to queue outside the City Bakeries although she was not then Hamlet's mother but the very young and talented actress Eileen Herlie. I looked for this film star eagerly but although often informed that she was a genuine artificial cream-cookie seeker, I never managed a confirmed sighting.

I have said that the queues were basically good-humoured, and they were but there was nothing of the *Pollyanna* about them. The women spent too much time standing in wind and sleet for that and they exercised a wary vigilance towards each other. Eyes darted round the shelves of the Co-op grocer's shop and watched the assistants for any under-the-counter sleight-of-hand. Was there rhubarb and ginger jam this week? Or was it all plum? Or did it matter anyway, since it was well known that it was made entirely from turnips and apples with a dash of spurious flavouring?

Strangely enough, the Minister of Food, Lord Woolton, was liked rather than otherwise. There was a feeling that he was genuinely trying to be fair. He was, we nodded sagely to each other in the queues, doing his best. You had under-the-counter deals, true, but Lord Woolton was trying to see that we all got fed. He had increased the rations last Christmas and it was only Japan's entry into the war that brought cheese back to two ounces a week, butter to two ounces and margarine to six ounces. Anyway, can you imagine how Jerry must be doing?

For those women standing in lines, clothes rationing was another constant problem. How did you balance a frock at seven coupons against a nightdress at six against corsets at three? Yet they could all find one coupon to spare for the young bride-to-be who had nothing in which to get married. Their husbands were equally generous with their spare coupons but the object of their benevolence was the local junior or senior football team which needed coupons for the purchase of playing kit. Even the Scotland side was in sore need of equipment. We read with amazement that the famous international footballer, Tommy Walker of Heart of Midlothian, had donated a complete set of his international jerseys so that his country could take the field decently attired.

Football was hanging on in spite of the war. Indeed, it was doing better than hanging on, it was recovering. By 1942 several senior clubs in the East of Scotland had resumed operations and the old, famous names of Aberdeen, East Fife, Dundee United, Raith Rovers, Dunfermline Athletic, appeared again in the Saturday evening papers.

Suddenly at going on 14 years of age, military service did not seem decades away, as indeed it wasn't—another four years would see one just about ready for the services. At school those boys who were slightly older had for the most part joined the Air Training Corps, which did not seem to do much apart from holding good dances and playing a very high standard of football indeed.

I was very interested in aircraft recognition and had begun to collect the beautiful Dinky Toy scale models of the time. I had a Spitfire and Hurricane of course, but the twin prides of my collection were a Short Sunderland Flying Boat and a Dornier bomber, magnificently sinister in its black paint and swastikas. My enthusiasm had reached such a pitch that the purchase of these aircraft had become the first claim upon my pocket money when they abruptly disappeared from the shops. No doubt they had disappeared into the capacious melting pots of Lord Beaverbrook, together with the park railings and saucepans.

At that remarkably impressionable age I tended to mimic for weeks afterwards any film or theatrical performance that had impressed me. My parents were remarkably forbearing about this, not so my brothers who regarded it as a kind of one-upmanship, the more so that Philip, even at the age of eight, had considerably greater powers of imitation. My Charles James Fox, modelled on the actor Robert Morley in the film *The Young Mr Pitt*, was ill-received. In vain did I deliver perfectly Morley's languid reply when George III sent to know on what day he might expect Fox's resignation: "Tell His Majesty on Judgement Day. No, that might be rather a busy day—the day after." The boys were not impressed, not even when I told them that Robert Donat had played Pitt (an excellent choice on the grounds of fragility alone) and that Phyllis Calvert had played Pitt's girlfriend, Clarissa Eden.

Some wartime restrictions we bore with fortitude. The cutting of the petrol ration and the consequent disappearance of private cars and delivery vans meant that our games of street football could proceed uninterrupted for hours at a stretch. Nor did the rationing of soap appear any dreadful imposition to us, although the following Christmas we were mortified when a friend of my mother's brought a Christmas present "for the boys". This was an unexpected source and we tore open the Christmas paper (sufficiently rare of itself by now) with impatient fingers. The sight of six bars of scented soap made it well-nigh hopeless for us to try to force the polite grimace which the gimlet eye of our mother demanded.

Did she, the friend, think we were dirty or something?

The rationing of soap was a good illustration of the nightmare of administration which a simple decision could create. What was to happen with miners at the pit-head? They would need a special soap ration. Again, Glasgow water was beautifully soft and excellent for lathering but what about the poor benighted Londoners with their appalling hard water? They too got an extra ration.

On a Sunday morning in November 1942 I was delivering papers in Newlands, noticing as I went that the *Sunday Pictorial* was no longer including the Russian lessons which it had enthusiastically launched following the German invasion of the USSR in June the year before. It was a calm, sunny Sabbath with church-goers walking to service and munition workers cycling to Weir's, the big factory in Cathcart. Suddenly a just-remembered sound filled the air, the peal of church bells. These had not been sounded for more than two years and indeed in 1940 we would have dreaded to hear them since it would have been the sign that the long-expected invasion was under way. Now, however, the bells rang to acclaim the landing of the Americans in North Africa. Rommel and the Afrika Korps were now caught between the Americans driving eastwards from Morocco and the British advancing west from Egypt. There could be, according to Captain Liddell Hart, Military Correspondent of the *Sunday Pictorial*, only one outcome. Over Sunday lunch we agreed with the good Captain and it was in a happy frame of mind that we heard Enoch tap dance in *Happidrome*.

The Axis leaders would get what was coming to them. They had failed to knock London out. Hadn't we just listened to *Hi Gang* with Bebe Daniels and Ben Lyon, introduced as coming "from a theatre in the heart of London"? And the other star of the show, Vic Oliver, was Churchill's son-in-law, so when he predicted a quick end to the war he must know what he was on about, eh?

From time to time in the queues we encountered young women, seldom in black but with the taut smile of the bereaved. The number of those killed on active service was still comparatively small; there was nothing like the slaughter of the First World War where regiments recruited extensively from the same locality had persistently assailed frontally positions which had long been prepared and fortified. Yet merchant seamen were being lost, and airmen were being shot down. Many families had to live with the dread which ours was mercifully spared.

Because the casualties were small, comparatively, and because we knew little of the horror of the Japanese prison camps or the fate which awaited gypsies and Jews in Europe, it was still possible even in 1942 to be semi-jocular about the enemy. Thus, a well-known Glasgow firm of gentlemen's outfitters, Rowan's, advertising a last pre-war consignment of suits pitched its sales point at the twin acceptabilities of bargain and patriotism. The suits retailed at £9-15s-0d each and prospective buyers were warned that "an offer such as this is not likely to recur for many a long day — certainly not until Winston, Franklin and Joe take the heil out of Hitler, Musso and Tojo". The wording was interesting to me even then. Winston, the dogged no-nonsense man, Franklin the scholar-saint and Joe, the bluff shrewd peasant. Of the others, I noted "Musso", the diminutive implying contempt rather than affection.

I made a note of something else from the newspapers of that year, as I raced up and down the tenement stairs, developing the sturdiest of legs in doing so. It was a sentence from a broadcast from the leader of the Vichy French, Marshal Pétain. The fact that he was quoted at all was what struck me as strange, for Pétain was a bad word, synonymous with Quisling and traitor. The kindest thing that anybody had to say about him was that in his eighties he had turned senile. And yet . . . there seemed little of senility or treachery in these words to his fellow-countrymen: "From the partial exile in which I live, from the semi-liberty which has been left me, I am trying to fulfil my duty."

It was, perhaps, more difficult to be jocular inside Europe.

Chapter Six

1943

THE new year began with the news of the German catastrophe at Stalingrad, the first occasion on which the Germans, as opposed to their allies the Italians, had suffered a major defeat. We were jubilant at school, none more so than a classmate of mine James Mills. We had a wall magazine in Class 2A and, as one whose literary efforts were normally praised, I was none too pleased when Tommy Stairs, principal teacher of English, rightly dismissed a soppy poem I had written about Kirn. I remember with shuddering, the last two lines:

> Thus we bow to Kirn and proudly hail
> Her as Queen of the Clyde.

The wrenching break from "hail" at the end of one line to "Her" at the beginning of the next is marvellously bad. Tommy Stairs could spot a dud well off and he preferred, even if I did not, the astringent commentary of James Mills — whom I subsequently and jealously christened "Dark Satanic" — on the state of play on the Eastern Front.

> Hitler, you are a fake,
> And you made a terrific mistake
> When into Russia you did run,
> But now the tide is on the turn
> And the Russians in your wake.

On the strength of this effusion and despite "you did run" Dark Satanic Mills acquired for a few weeks the status of a minor prophet.

The British public was extremely pro-Russian at the time and as a token of the regard of the British public for the heroic defenders of Stalingrad, a special ceremonial sword of honour was made for the city and shown to the people of Britain before being sent to Russia.

The newspapers of the time made a great fuss of the event, particularly the *Daily Express*, which leads me now to think that it may have been a Beaverbrook idea. Perhaps a little piece of the Queen's Park gates or one of Mrs McGregor's saucepans is for ever Stalingrad. In one of his novels Evelyn Waugh wrote scornfully of the long shuffling lines of drab civilians queueing up in London to gawp at the Sword but at the time people thought it was a well-deserved tribute to a gallant and enduring ally.

Momentous international events and the trivia of the daily wartime existence continued to enlace in the most tangled fashion. Thus, the final Allied breakthrough in North Africa, with the capture of the seaports of Sfax and Bizerta, is inseparably linked with displays given by the School of Dancing which my brothers and sisters attended.

My mother had enrolled Julie and Kathleen (later) in the Sadie Simpson School of Dancing, specialising in ballet, tap and acrobatic dancing. While attending classes with them one day, my mother discovered that Miss Simpson was in need of a pianist to play at rehearsals and indeed at performances. It was a fortunate turn of events for both women. My mother had been a pianist in a dance band in the 1920s, and could play any piece of music at sight, or for that matter, transpose it. Her hands were becoming ever more arthritic but she persevered for the twin reasons that she was under instructions to keep her fingers moving if she could, and the fact that the playing, although physically so agonising that she was often reduced to tears, gave her an interest and sense of purpose which nothing else could have done.

She helped to organise and discipline the classes. The mothers were frequently those most in need of discipline and she threw herself into the work of preparing shows or displays as they were called. Frank and Philip were conscripted to give some kind of counterbalance to the overwhelming mass of girls who took part in the shows. Phil was a very confident dancer with a good stage presence while Frank had ability but felt his exposed position keenly.

I managed to avoid being drafted for dancing, being a notoriously stiff-rumped mover, but allowed myself to be talked into doing a solo piano spot during the shows. This was a grievous error as I was quite simply not good enough to do so and it was surprising that I should have gone on, since in most things I had a sound and objective assessment of my own capabilities. There may have been an element of not wanting to let the Shawlands branch of the Von Trapp family down, but it was an error. Had I been a good sight reader, I could have been of some use at rehearsals but I was then as poor a sight reader as my mother was a good one. None of this deterred me from inflicting a severely mutilated, simplified and embarrassing version of the Tschaikowski *Piano Concerto No. 1* upon an astonished audience during the Christmas show in the Lyric Theatre.

The audience may rightly have been astonished but I ploughed on blithely and I suppose that it did make a change from the interminable dancing. The printed programme for a display by the Sadie Simpson School of Dancing was a daunting sight. There might well be 60 items for every pupil, no matter how ungifted, had to have her hour on stage. Item 29, Russian Festival, in which two dozen pre-pubescent girls pranced around in red knee-boots—wellies which had undergone a blood transfusion—was never markedly different from Item 41, Polish Festival, in which a different but similarly shod two dozen galumphed about the stage.

Had I confined myself to indifferent piano playing all might have been well, but I lacked the steel to hold out against the suggestion that I should play Santa Claus in the Dance of the Christmas Toys. No parent could be found who was fool enough to volunteer for the part — many fathers saw field service or overtime as a blessed excuse — and although I asserted that I was too small for the part, counting my lack of inches for once as a blessing, I was as big as there was available. I therefore took the stage of the excellent little Lyric Theatre in Sauchiehall Street and, dressed as Santa Claus, pretended to wind up four tots with a mechanical rattle while reciting an appalling couplet of my own devising:

> I am Santa Claus, I am king of the toys,
> And I have lots of presents for good little girls and boys.

Many years ago the Lyric building was demolished to make way for an office block but until it was I used to hurry past it with ducked head and reddened face. It was not our only venue, however, as the Sadie Simpson School of Dancing visited various hospitals where we danced remorselessly at convalescing ex-servicemen. This led to a memorable incident, although I simply recount it as I was elsewhere that night. The troupe had danced for British wounded at Cowglen Military Hospital and had finished the performance when the matron asked if the children would consider dancing for the

German wounded and prisoners who were there. Miss Simpson agreed at once, the most generous of acts since her husband was Jewish, and the Germans watched entranced. It was later realised that they had not seen children in a normal situation for months, perhaps years. At the end of it all, a spokesman said that they wanted to give the dancers something in return but that all they had was their coffee, which was by no means good. However they hoped the children would drink it as a hope for a better future and a sign of thanks. The coffee came in tin mugs and Julie did not like coffee but the message in my mother's eyes was unmistakable — "You will drink it and you will say you like it."

I was slightly sorry to have missed this performance as I had a notion of a pretty 13-year-old, Phamie Toner, who sang *Bless This House* in a thin true voice which complemented her ethereal face. My fancy cooled when I heard her snarl "Paws off, you!" to another and more daring youth.

In the early summer of 1943 we returned late one night from visiting another hospital with the show. It was very late and Julie, who was not quite five, was already fast asleep as we came in, the audience and the excitement having exhausted her. We switched on the wireless to hear that Tunisia had fallen to the Allies and that the Afrika Korps had effectively surrendered.

Within a few weeks the invasion of Sicily was under way and Peter Kane, a friend of my father's, delivered his opinion that "Musso'll get his, now". Peter was typical of many Scots of his time in that he had nothing like the same contempt for Hitler, thought indeed that the latter was right in the laws that he had passed against the Jews. The full horror of what was happening in Europe was yet veiled from us, and Peter, kindest of men, could have been depended upon to succour any individual Jew, but it was nevertheless a chilling thing to hear.

By the time the Sicilian invasion was in full swing, we were back at Kirn. The great convoys were now assembling at the Tail of the Bank off Gourock. The great Cunarders, the *Queen Mary* and the *Queen Elizabeth*, the battleships *Nelson* and *Rodney* and other capital ships were frequent visitors. Stealthily, just before dusk and the closing of the submarine boom which stretched from the Cloch lighthouse to Dunoon the great ships would slip away to the open sea, the *Queens* capable of transporting thousands of soldiers at a time.

This was the summer when, by accident, I took up golf. Among the new boys visiting Kirn was a fair-haired 13-year-old who was even stockier than myself and who also, thank God, wore short trousers. I had begun to think that with the exception of my great friend Pat Harrigan, who wore shorts with the conscious eccentricity of someone who was 5 feet 11 inches tall, I was perhaps the last schoolboy in short trousers in the western world. My mother stated that she had a great objection to making me a "wee cut-down man" so shorts it was. Alan, bless him, also wore shorts and after the inevitable verbal sparring and speiring of first acquaintance, said to me, "Do you play golf?" The answer to that question was "No", but since I had understood him to say, "Do you play goal?", to which the answer was "Yes", I nodded my head in affirmation and fixed a meeting with him next morning. I turned up accoutred for football to find this strongly built, low-slung boy carrying golf clubs.

This was awkward, for I didn't play and even if I did Frank and Phil would perforce be excluded. However, with an ill-enough grace, I accompanied Alan up Ardenslate Road to the high part of Kirn where the Cowal Golf Club was located. He was something new in our experience, a sportsman who was not remotely interested in association football. He was marvellously acrobatic and was in fact to become one of the finest gymnasts ever produced by Jordanhill College, the headquarters of the Scottish School of Physical Recreation. Observation would have suggested that with his build he was destined to have been a scrum-half and observation would have been right. When golf was over he would line us up in the long grass beside the putting green and teach us by demonstration the correct method of rugby tackling. The sensation is still vivid of bracing oneself for the tackle from behind and yet being invariably slightly surprised by it.

His pre-eminent skill though was in golf. I was to be instructed, had I but known it, by a future champion of Hamilton Golf Club. He stood up, addressed the ball on the first tee, swung and the ball hurtled away, quite low, and bounded along the fairway. I was snared and again my objectivity let me down. My credo where sport was concerned was that there was no game I could not master, did I but choose to devote my energies to it. This simple creed was indeed erroneous but many a man has followed a false belief with total conviction.

Whether I mastered the game or not, I would need equipment. I had no clubs and in any case their manufacture had all but stopped by now. It was difficult enough to get golf balls — the professional received perhaps two dozen remoulds each month and members clearly had priority. We haunted the wooden clubhouse day and night, camping out on the verandah and occasionally the pro would sell us a golf ball, almost certainly to get rid of our begging faces. We also, playing from the same bag, combed the rough. Alan did it because it was essential to find golf balls, I did it because I was there anyway.

On one of my excursions to the more remote and improbable parts of the course I came across an almost brand-new Silver King with its distinctive square dimples. Rapture, but rapture most fleeting! I made one solid connection with Alan's mid-iron and the Silver King abdicated, disintegrated. It had obviously mouldered through two or three wartime winters and was all too literally a whited sepulchre.

How to get money for clubs, or at least to be seen to make a start in that direction, for my parents were very generous when their children were seen to be making an effort? For that matter, how to get money for this holiday we were now entered upon? The answer was simple. I would enter and win the Talent Competition which was held every afternoon in the Castle Gardens, Dunoon. It was a "Go As You Please" for youngsters and youngsters were liberally interpreted as anyone up to and including 16 years old. The winner had ten shillings lavished upon him.

The competition occupied the last half hour or so of the afternoon dance band concert. The band, a perfectly adequate ensemble, would alternate *Poet and Peasant* with novelty numbers and current war songs which varied with the state of the great campaign. It might be *The Navy's Here* which commemorated the freeing of British merchant sailors from the German prison ship *Altmark*, or the tribute to the RAF, *Lords of the Air*, with its final chorus sung rousingly by a young crooner of military age:

> Lord of the Heavens above
> Answer my prayer,
> Long rule Britannia's sons
> Lords of the Air.

All went well. I skated through my heat on the Tuesday afternoon playing a composition called *March of the Indians*, a piece of rubbish full of notes and fury and musically worthless. The opposition was non-existent and was not strong even in the final on Friday. Finals were held on Friday because people went home on the Saturday, which was known in the coastal resorts as change-over day.

There were only two possible threats to the ten-shilling note among the other seven turns. One was a Phamie Toner-like creature who warbled *Johnny Doughboy found a rose in Ireland* and who was well received but not ecstatically so. But if low comedy was your taste then Eugene might pose a threat. Eugene was chubby, carrot-haired, unlovely, stentorian and he sang *Der Fuehrer's Face*.

> When Der Fuehrer says "We are the master race",
> We Heil! . . . Heil! . . . right in der Fuehrer's face
> Not to love Der Fuehrer is a great disgrace
> So we Heil! . . . Heil! . . . right in Der Feuhrer's face.

The gaps after the Heil!s were filled by the singer blowing rasp-berries as loudly as he could, which in Eugene's case was remarkably loudly. He got a big hand but I had been gazing round the curtains from the wings and noted that while the groundlings were whistling and cheering the respectable matrons were much less enthusiastic and there were a lot of respectable matrons.

I had the advantage of going on last and I clattered through the dreadful *March of the Indians* with the sublime confidence of the basically untalented. There could only be one winner and I received my prize from the MC who was not, as might have been expected, the bandleader but the manager of the Winter Gardens, a white-haired Kentucky colonel kind of man.

My master plan had worked but not that of the Allies in Italy. It had started well with Sicily falling before the end of our holiday and indeed Italy itself surrendered. Peter Kane's prophecy was apparently being very rapidly fulfilled as "Musso" was deposed, imprisoned in Ponza and replaced by Marshal Badoglio who at once entered into negotiations with the Allies. Surely it couldn't be long now?

Or could it? Within a fortnight the Germans were claiming that Mussolini had been liberated from his prison and was back with his family. We laughed at this latest monstrous lie from Dr Goebbels and waited for our own government to contradict it. We waited . . . and waited. Eventually came a shamefaced admission that indeed the *Duce* was free and that he had resumed political power.

The autumn of 1943 was a low point for me in my miniscule world. I disgraced myself at the school Harvest Camp, my attempts to make the school team failed, it was becoming obvious that I lacked any vestige of mathematical ability and Bill, my oldest and best friend, was moving to Aberdeen. The mathematical stupidity was the least of my afflictions as neither then nor since have I felt the remotest attraction to the subject but the teaching staff were very aware that this failure on my part might severely restrict career prospects. With an irritating lack of logic they proclaimed that since I was outstanding in two or three other subjects, notably English and History, I should be able to cope with Mathematics. No amount of telling them that I *liked* English and History could budge them from this lunatic certainty of theirs.

They would not believe that my terror of geometry was such that I learned theorems word for word. Pupils were then and for some time afterwards required to write out from memory the long proofs of geometrical theorems. When I say that they might as well have been in Sanskrit that is not quite true; they would have been better in Sanskrit as I had some ability in languages. As it was, when proving the congruency of triangles — and who wanted to, for God's sake? — I would mutter incantations such as CAB=FED which I thought of as cab=fed, a taxi being fuelled. If in the examination the triangles were set as PQR and XYZ, a nasty sneaking habit which was all too prevalent, I had no mnemonics and I was floored. Still, as I cordially loathed Maths, my inability to do it was momentarily embarrassing in class but of no greater significance than that.

Bill's going to Aberdeen was infinitely more serious. His father was a civil servant with the Ministry of Labour and had been promoted to the northern city, had indeed been living there for several months. Now it was time for the whole family to move. We were grief-stricken. Bill, a dedicated Glaswegian, did not want to go and we did not want him to go. He was my oldest friend; there was no one with whom I felt more comfortable. He and his father had season tickets for Ibrox and when his father moved to Aberdeen I fell heir to his ticket and would go along to the Rangers games with Bill. On one occasion I was in the invidious position of vehemently supporting Queen's Park from the reserved seats of the home side.

Bill was inextricably linked with my football. He was a member of the Queen's Park School under-14 football team at a time when that school produced senior players in droves. Bill would later sign for Rangers and even then was a wing-half in the classical Scottish mould. I was not the goalkeeper of the Holyrood under-14 side which was due to play Queen's Park in November in what was to be Bill's last match before becoming a pupil of Robert Gordon's

College, in Aberdeen. In all fairness I should have kept goal for our under-14s, but I was small and in the eyes of our games master "Spud" Murphy, the deficiency in inches was not compensated for by good handling and positional sense. Instead, the Holyrood goal was entrusted to Ted Myles, an amiable beanstalk but not a goal-keeper. In the trials I had played one of those matches one dreams about, held everything and brought off a great smother at the centre-forward's feet.

Spud, however, was not impressed. An amiable, hearty man he was not one of football's great thinkers and analysts. His instruction to us was confined to an injunction to "keep your knee over the ball" when shooting and he seemed disappointingly uninclined to take the field on those Games Days when the rain fell. In his book, big fellows kept goal.

On the Friday morning at interval time I hurried down to the gym to confirm my selection on the notice-board. There was the Under-14 team and I needed to look no further than the first name: Myles. We had two periods of French thereafter and in the course of them I continually and savagely snubbed an excellent girl, Mae Smith, whom I had been cultivating. She looked puzzled and hurt as well she might have done. I hoped for a disabling bout of sickness for my rival and turned up on the Saturday morning with my boots but so did Ted.

Over the weeks the tall Ted retained his place, our forwards usually managing to score as many goals as he lost. The week before we were due to meet Queen's Park we played John Street, a renowned football school also, and drew 4-4. By the most charitable of interpretations, and mine was scarcely that, the Myles boy should have saved two of the goals. Surely even "Spud", not the greatest judge of a player ever born, would see the error of his ways? "Spud" did no such thing. He stuck by his original selection and Queen's Park also achieved a 4-4 draw. I hadn't the courage or humility to attend that game. I would have given anything to play against Bill at inter-school level and now I never would. He went off to Aberdeen and with him went a fair slice of my past. We said we would write and, against probability I suppose, we did, regularly and at length.

It was not a good time for courage where I was concerned and the Harvest Camp escapade at Perth was another fiasco. By this stage of the war schools had seen summer holidays cut to a month and the time saved was reallocated to October when schools helped with the harvest. The senior pupils, fifth and sixth year, brought in the grain from such places as Dufftown in Banffshire while the middle school was destined for the potato-gathering—the "tattie-howking" in the vivid Scots phrase.

Where pupils were concerned it was a job for volunteers. With regard to teachers that was the theory also, but in reality the education authority leaned quite heavily on them and was not above hinting that promotion prospects might be enhanced or otherwise according to the location of those same teachers come the autumn break.

I pestered my mother to be allowed to go, but she had misgivings. She pointed out that I had shown no fondness for manual labour and that my one brush with the soil, the lettuce-growing, could hardly be categorised as successful. Nor, she reminded me, were any of my close school friends going. Pat Harrigan had uttered an aristocratic moan of horror when I floated the idea. He informed me that it had taken the hard work of four generations of Harrigans to escape the potato fields once and for all and he was not so ungrateful as to throw that hard work back in their face. My father, however, was an unexpectedly powerful advocate. "Let the boy go, Kitty," he kept saying. Later I realised that this was one of his few excursions into the sardonic. He had, after all, frequently howked tatties and it was an experience which he was very anxious that I should have.

On a bright October Friday, 150 of us crowded on to an already packed train that soon afterwards steamed out of Buchanan Street railway station for Perth, which after Glasgow came as a revelation. The shops seemed better stocked, the air was clearer and cleaner and the grey stone houses by the river were very handsome. Our billet, however, was of red sandstone, the Northern Primary School, which was situated just along the road from Muirton Park, the ground of St Johnstone Football Club. St Johnstone had closed down for the duration of war but that mattered not. At the first chance I got I put my eye to a gap in the fence and beheld the playing area. No Israelite spy ever got a greater kick from seeing Canaan than I had from the vision of Muirton. I had seen St Johnstone's ground, just as on the way up, in passing through Stirling, I had seen the ground of King's Park Football Club. To be more accurate I had seen what used to be the ground, for a lone German aircraft had jettisoned its bombs on King's Park's grandstand back in 1941. That was a real war crime.

The English principal, Tom Stairs, was in charge of the operation and we were issued immediately with palliasses and pillows. These we took to classrooms which had been cleared of desks and we were assigned, a dozen scholars to each room. There was still light for a game of football in the school playground which was large enough to permit the use of a full-sized ball and was marred only by the presence of a large and intrusive tree which had to be played round and through. One or two of the staff joined in our game, notably Jack McGuire, who had played with Queen's Park and was an excellent winger, and Sandy McDougall, who had not and was not. Sandy, appropriately one might think, was a Scottish Nationalist. We were to see him the next day, kilted and bonneted, as he harangued a glazed audience on the North Inch. Judging by the frequency of his references to the "English war" it might be suspected that Sandy was a pressed man at the potato digging.

The gathering dusk drove us in from football to supper, mince followed by semolina, both of an equal sloppiness and chiefly distinguished from each other by colour rather than consistency or taste. The next two days were fine as we were not working. We marvelled at the up-to-date swimming baths which Perth possessed and heard Alice Faye sing *You'll never know* throatily in a film about San Francisco.

Sunday was church parade to St John's, an escorted walk along the river and, in the evening, a concert. Perth was a garrison town even in peacetime, being the regimental depot of the Black Watch and in 1943 it was stiff with soldiers. The concert party which entertained us was a military one and a corporal in the ATS attracted wolf whistles as she sang *Roses of Picardy*. We didn't like the song very much but my fellow-agriculturals were much more taken with *Hutsut Brolsom*. This was a kind of nonsense song though not so overtly nonsensical as *Mairzy Doats and Dozy Doats* (Mares eat oats and Does eat oats). Gracie Fields had introduced *Hutsut* when she came back in the middle of the war to Britain from the United States. Her going had caused some hostility, even although it subsequently emerged that she had gone at the request of our Government to raise funds. Nevertheless her popularity suffered and she would have recovered lost ground more quickly perhaps by singing her pre-war favourites such as *The biggest aspidistra in the world* and *Turn Herbert's face to the wall, Mother,* instead of what sounded like gibberish.

That first audience listened baffled as did we, concluding that those Yanks had corrupted Our Gracie. The concert party had jugglers, impressionists who did Abbott and Costello and an accordionist who played *The Miles to Dundee* and *We're no awa' to bide awa'*. *The Miles to Dundee* may with hindsight have been *The Crooked Bawbee* but it was something everybody could join in singing.

In the interests of audience involvement and with mistaken generosity, the troupers invited us to do "turns" and two of our number rendered *Pistol Packin' Mama* and *Comin' In on a Wing and a Prayer* while I nipped in with the durable *March of the Indians*. Cleared off to bed at ten o'clock we told jokes that certainly did nothing for holy purity although a farting competition never got off the ground.

On the Monday morning we breakfasted on porridge and a dry roll with an even drier slice of square sausage. Then we paraded for allocation of sites. Our squad were informed that they were to work on Hill of Ruthven farm, owned by a Mr McGillivray and, each of us clutching a packet of sandwiches, we boarded a ricketty lorry which lurched off along the Dunkeld Road in the general direction of Stanley.

It was bright, windy and cold as we spilled from the lorry and began our apprenticeship as potato pickers. The field was divided into lengths or "drills" marked out by sticks, and the tractor raced round the field turning up potatoes by the hundred. We filled the wicker baskets with an enthusiasm which owed everything to novelty. The grieve, or overseer, kept stalking round, exhorting us to "Make a clean pick". He had an eye of astonishing keenness for even the most fugitive potato.

The tractor made its second circuit. We picked. It came again. We picked. It was becoming more painful to straighten. There were local women with us in the field who picked with a practised economy of motion. The stark realisation dawned. There was nothing else to this job. The tractor would keep coming round and we would keep gathering, perhaps 20 times in a morning.

Lunch came at last, strong tea and sandwich spread, an anaemic vegetable concoction on our bread. There was a fierce short blatter of rain then we resumed picking. The afternoon crawled past until it was time to clamber up on the lorry, looking to sit directly behind the cabin out of the wind. Mince and semolina again at the Northern Primary School was our portion and the absence of off-colour jokes at night denoted extreme fatigue rather than any marked access of morality.

The second and last day for me was noteworthy for my first taste of industrial action. We were far from being as patriotic as we should have been. Our thoughts should have been on the nation's larder, which we were helping to fill, aiding the fulfilment of the Government's expressed desire, "Eat less bread, eat potatoes instead". Our thoughts should have been so, but we were much more exercised by what we took to be sharp practice on the part of the farmer. It seemed to me that the drills were longer than they had been on the previous day. We were good at judging distances — penalty areas and cricket pitches were our everyday currency. I mentioned my thoughts to "Quadie", my next in line. He took a look and agreed. We canvassed other side-of-mouth opinions like convicts in a James Cagney movie. There was unanimity. Also, to our partial eyes, the tractor driver was coming round faster than he had done the previous day. We had more to do and less time in which to do it. It was not to be borne. It was during the lunch-break that some forgotten genius, over the cheese sandwiches, conceived the idea of bunging a small potato up the tractor exhaust. This unpatriotic action gained us an hour's remission while the trouble was diagnosed and a court of enquiry conducted.

By the time we got back to our potatoes I had decided to quit. I had seen the train from Aberdeen pass a couple of fields away, heading for Glasgow and I thought that before long I would be on it. A fortnight's repetitive labour, punctuated by bad food, was not my definition of a holiday. I would simply go, as I did not want Tommy Stairs or anyone else to talk me out of my decision. So it was that, like a thief in the night, or a chapter from John Buchan's *Book of Escapes and Hurried Journeys* which I had prophetically brought with me, I crept through the blacked-out streets of Perth and boarded a train for Glasgow. It was imaginative, showed a praiseworthy initiative and was totally irresponsible. I had literally vanished into the mirk leaving Tommy Stairs, responsible for me in fact and in law, totally ignorant of my movements.

Completing my journey by tramcar, I regained the house in Deanston Drive just short of midnight. My father smiled quietly, my mother was overtly scornful as was Frank, holidaying with relations down in Newcastle. "Big quitter", his postcard inelegantly but forcefully said. There was no riposte I could properly make whether to my mother, to Frank or to Tommy Stairs when on the first day back at school he returned my ration book to me with icy politeness. I shrugged it off as if it didn't matter but I never subsequently failed to carry out a tour of duty.

It was well for the national interest that some members of the family had a stricter construction of the word "duty". Our two sea-going members of the family were Frank McNaughton and Jack Murphy, both cousins, although in deference to age the former was known to us as Uncle Frank. He was by far the most glamorous of our relations and had been at sea before the war as an officer with the Merchant Navy, coming ashore in the late 1930s to work in his home town of Liverpool with Crawford's, the big biscuit firm. On one of his pre-war visits to Glasgow he had called for us at school in his little green sports car, thereby raising our stock considerably. Now he was a lieutenant-commander on board a corvette, the *Zamalek*, and was in the throes of a difficult war which saw him in the North Atlantic at the height of the U-boat campaigns and later on the long and terrifyingly arduous Arctic convoys to Murmansk. We listened avidly as he told of a cold so intense that if anyone fell in the water, his name tag was salvaged rather than the person himself. He was particularly critical of the chilly welcome which the crews received after battling through to Murmansk, an aloofness which bordered on hostility.

We picked up one friendly Russian for our family, however. While in Russia the ship's cat had kittens which were named Zam and Alek after the ship. We fell heir to Alek but although we took to him from the start we felt that Alek was rather a nondescript name for a cat. As he soon distinguished himself by his cupboard-leaping talents and his agility in goal against a paper ball, he became Alek Tarzan and answered happily to it for the rest of his days.

Frank McNaughton was multi-talented and infinitely stimulating. He drew well, left-handed, and had had cartoons published in service magazines. He did his best to teach me about angles of refraction and in between he told me about such heroes as Cyril Washbrook and Eddie Paynter of Lancashire and Dixie Dean of Everton. This last was very broad-minded of him for he was and remained a Liverpool supporter. His loyalty to Merseyside as a whole over-rode this and of all the players he mentioned it was another Evertonian that I felt most anxious to see, the oddly named Pongo Waring. Frank's wife Joyce who was pretty and whom we liked came to stay with us for a while when the *Zamalek's* home base was the Clyde.

He was particularly good at encouraging interests. About this time he took me into John Smith's, the largest Glasgow bookshop, and invited me to pick any book I fancied. It was an expensive offer, for my choice, as I later found to my horror, although printed on inferior wartime paper, cost twelve shillings and sixpence, a small fortune. Frank never blenched and the book he provided, D C Somervell's *A Short History of the United States to 1941*, remains in my judgement the best short-compass work on the period and subject.

From Frank we learned of such things as holystone, the points of the compass and Carley floats. He did not share Will Fyffe's romantic notion of Clydeside shipyard workers, having been kept from patrol once for the best part of a week while two shipyard unions debated which should drill a hole through a metal-covered wooden rail. He was sharp, witty and generous and the generosity he held in common with Jack Murphy, but Jack was a gentler soul, the personification of good nature. Before joining the Merchant Navy he had been a keen Rover Scout. I incline to think that he brought his virtues to the movement rather than that the latter conferred them on him. It was typical of him that when he sailed on a tanker he worried that he was being paid perceptibly more than the Royal Navy seamen who guarded him and that when he was transferred to a Norwegian tanker, he worried that he was paid very much more again since Scandinavian rates of pay for seamen were much higher. Others would have argued that there wasn't enough money in the universe to remunerate anyone who spent his waking and sleeping hours aboard a gigantic firebomb. Certainly Frank was adamant that he wouldn't have had Jack's job for a fortune. Jack was torpedoed but fortunately in the milder latitudes of the Caribbean and was picked up after a not too uncomfortable (his words) few hours in the water.

The two used to argue good-humouredly over the respective virtues of the Royal and Merchant navies and the Scottish and English international football teams. There could be very little argument about the second topic for the superiority of English wartime football was undeniable. Wartime internationals followed a predictable pattern for us which took the following shape.

We presented ourselves at Hampden Park about one o'clock. If the weather was wet, and it often was, we came by train and rendezvous'd with Bill. If it was a good day we came on foot, playing football all the way along the banks of the River Cart. It was quicker to come over Langside Monument Brae but much too steep and busy for football. We played a game called "Combination" with a tennis ball and when one of us brought off a dexterous flick or header or delivered a pass of outstanding accuracy, the correct form was to murmur "Helluva nice", one of our more daring phrases. I employed it more than the other two boys and when we fell out, they would sometimes threaten to denounce me at home for my use of it.

Once inside the ground, we got as near to the front as we could. Our great dread was that a six-foot-nine-inch Grenadier Guardsman would come and stand in front of us. Fortunately, these were thin on the ground and on their infrequent appearances, very punctilious about letting us stand in front of them. The time dragged, not greatly helped by the community singing — number four on your songsheets, lads — although Elliott Dobie, the famous Scottish singer, tried hard to whip up national fervour as he stood white-sweatered on the rostrum. Of all the songs, only one, *The Bonny Wells o' Wearie*, stays in my mind. It lodges there because it was so dirge-like, an all-too-frequently apt prediction of our performance, and because I never heard it anywhere else although it was an annual inclusion in the Hampden repertoire. The singing over, pipe bands marched briskly across the ground, droning remorselessly before retiring in good order up the sloped running track at the side of the stand. The teams were then presented to the Duke of Gloucester or General Montgomery or Lady Churchill or some such dignitary and while it was no doubt a considerable thrill for the players, we boys found the string of introductions irksome in the extreme.

At last came the National Anthem, even in wartime often exhausting the patience of the crowd, so that the roar of anticipation began to growl in the last two bars. Then the kick-off, and the English in their billowing white shirts which gave a curious impression of broadness, would run amok. They didn't always win of course — they had lost 5-4 in a memorable match in 1942 — but now a year later they demolished Scotland. Their marvellous right wing of Stanley Matthews and Raich Carter shredded the Scots defence and behind them the half-backs, Cliff Britton, Stan Cullis and Joe Mercer, played the polished, intelligent football that we had been brought up to believe was purely and peculiarly Scottish. On that April day in 1943 we got off lightly at 4-0.

Of course we knew why we had lost, we muttered darkly as we hid in a passage at the Mount Florida end of the ground after the match. We were hiding because there was to be a Scottish Junior Cup semi-final that same evening and we didn't see why we should have to pay for admission twice. So we ate our sandwiches, skulked and kept watch. We had lost because all the best Scottish players were away at the war, knee-deep in jungle ferns, tossing on the North Atlantic or even at that very moment flying over the Ruhr. The English side, it was well known on the other hand, were not allowed to be sent further than ten miles from Aldershot, so it stood to reason that they would win, didn't it? What had the comedian said in the last Alhambra pantomime? The English would fight to the last Scotsman.

It was a comforting notion and we cherished it fiercely but it owed more to wishful thinking than to reality. Most of the pre-war players of Rangers and Celtic were still available to the Scottish selectors even in 1943 since the war record of neither club was at all distinguished. Other noted Scottish internationals such as Tommy Walker of Hearts and Jimmy Carabine of Third Lanark were certainly on call for much the greater part of the war. We preferred the conspiracy theory to the actuality, not daring to admit that the English had thrashed us because they were far and away the better side.

The Christmas of 1943 had some claim to be the dreariest of the war. Unlike the four previous wartime Christmases, it had become too far to look back, while a year later we would be firmly lodged in Europe and the end would be at hand. There were now pratically no toys in the shops, the Hornby trains and the mechanical wonders of 1939 had long gone, there were no dolls worth looking at and such toys as there were appeared to be hewn from crude wooden blocks. I felt very sorry for Julie and Kathleen, for at least we, the boys, had known better and more opulent days.

Peter Kane came to the rescue. From somewhere he found material to make a magnificent doll's house, resplendent in red roughcast. The delicacy of the tiny pieces of furniture was a testimony to the man's astonishing craftsmanship and the little wardrobes, beds and chests of drawers were brought to a burnished perfection by his wife, Beck, who had been a French polisher to trade before becoming a stewardess with the Anchor line. There was even a battery which operated a lighting system and this house at least required no black-out material. It would have been a magnificent present even in peacetime and Peter and Beck had the satisfaction that never was a doll's house longer or more intensively played with.

As befited the dignity of the eldest son, an eldest son who had now reached the age of 13, I was allowed to attend Midnight Mass on my own for the first time. I climbed the steep hill to St Mary's, Pollokshaws, through the darkness and sleety rain to the stuffy, well-lit church. There were some servicemen there but not too many. Scots tended to take their leave over New Year if they had any choice in the matter. Still, there were sufficient Army, Navy and Air Force uniforms around with wives and girlfriends on their arms to make it a joyful occasion, or perhaps more accurately a comparatively joyful occasion. My history books were dotted with references to Thirty Years' Wars, Seven Years' Wars and even Hundred Years' Wars and there seemed no good reason why this current one should not give them all a run for their money.

Chapter Seven

1944:
Praise the Lord and pass the ammunition

IN January 1944 we appeared to have reached the classic stalemate of the elephant in combat with the whale. The Allies were bogged down in Italy, the Germans, despite Stalingrad were holding on . . . just . . . on the Eastern Front and still had the occasional local offensive left in them. The war against Japan went on, bloody, apparently unsuccessful, comparatively unreported. Only the huge numbers of Americans now visible on the streets and the incessant activities at ports and railway stations gave the sign that anything momentous was in the offing.

The civilian population was flagging. We were four and a half years into the war by now and it was beginning to show. Almost every day brought some new deprivation, trivial in itself and not to be remotely compared with what our servicemen were enduring but depressing, stamina-sapping, psychologically damaging. If the Government said that lopping five inches off the length of men's socks was going to defeat Hitler then we must suppose that they knew best and for like reason we would accept the disappearance of high heels, more especially we who did not wear them, but cause and effect could not always be immediately connected. Crepe soles and heels went, clogs came in, turbans were everywhere.

Bread had grown steadily darker during the war until now it was almost black. Crampsey bread was blacker than most when it arrived home for by this time the waxed wrapping paper of pre-war days had disappeared and the loaf was presented to the customer unadorned. As we usually called in for bread on our way back from one of our interminable games of football or bouts of tracking, our hands were normally rather repulsive and we managed to transfer a fair portion of soil to the plain or pan loaf. The black bread could be put to other uses. Pool petrol had been given a coloured additive so that the authorities would be able to tell if anyone was using unauthorised fuel. Many people, a cousin of ours in Bishopton included, discovered that this coloured additive could be removed if the petrol was strained through bread.

It was difficult to keep my mind on these important happenings because I had at long last made the school team. Passing the gymnasium one Thursday afternoon I had looked up at the notice-board through sheer force of habit and there I was, R A Crampsey, listed in goal to play against St Mark's in the Glasgow and District Schools League, Fourth Division. The game was to be at Shettleston and we were to meet at the school at 9 a.m.

By five o'clock in the morning I was grimly awake and sitting up in a living-room chair. I left the house at seven o'clock and was at the school before eight, spending the next hour in a ceaseless perambulation of the block. We drew 2-2 and I had a fair enough game, a slight question mark over the first goal but two good saves to be put into the other scale by way of counterpoise. It was never-theless a nervy few days until I read the following week that I had retained my place against John Street and this time I did play badly, being as undistinguished as the rest of us as we were hammered 4-2. The following game was the return match against Bill's school, Queen's Park, and although he had gone I was desperate to play, but without any real hopes of doing so.

Spud Murphy partially redeemed himself in my eyes by keeping faith with his goalkeeper, although in truth my previous week's display had been every bit as bad as one or two of those of Ted Myles. He should probably have dropped me but I reflected on the previous times when he should certainly have picked me. I decided to forgive him, at least partially. When in future years I was picked to play for Scotland at Hampden and Spud came round to remind me of his connection with me in early days, I would graciously bestow on him a complimentary ticket for the enclosure. I was not quite magnanimous enough to make it one for the stand.

We played Queen's Park in the Recreation Ground. They were one of the strongest of the Glasgow schools and had a particularly attractive green-and-gold hooped strip. It was therefore very much against expectation and the form book when we managed to win 3-2 before a gratifyingly large crowd. I hastened to acquaint Bill by letter of this famous victory although I would infinitely rather have played against him in October and lost heavily. In his reply he indicated that he thought that Queen's Park's performances must have deteriorated since he had gone north and in the last sentence asked if Frank, Philip and I would like to spend the Easter holidays with him in Aberdeen. It was a rhetorical question if ever there was one.

Bill came down to spend a few days with us over Easter and we travelled back up north with him. We arrived late at Buchanan Street Station, reaching it just five minutes before the train was due to go. Bill's mother, Aunt Betty, had managed to keep four seats for us, a great feat of courage at that stage of the war. We enjoyed the journey north and were captivated by Aberdeen although we had never in our lives been so cold. We rode the trams from Bridge of Dee to Bridge of Don, played football at Hazlehead and laughed ourselves sick at such names at Burnieboozle. The sing-song voices of the local children were a fertile field for Phil's mimicry and we went twice to a cinema in Rosemount where one of the records was of a player piano banging out *Let's all go down the Strand*.

We were surprised at the amount of bomb damage which was in evidence but were told that although Aberdeen had not been subjected to any one attack on the Clydebank or Greenock scale, there had been continuous light and medium-heavy raids almost since the very outbreak of war. One relic of peacetime days was the University Rag Day, what had been known in Glasgow as Charities Day. Our own city had not seen one of these since 1940 but the Aberdeen students had clearly kept going, although we thought their slogan, "Who is Yehudi?" was feeble indeed. Still, the sight of the lorries with their tableaux revived one pre-war memory and the Saturday morning parade was a fine curtain-raiser for our visit to Pittodrie in the afternoon to see Aberdeen take on Raith Rovers.

Then it was time to go back south, having extorted a promise from Bill's mother that she would let him come down to Kirn to join us in July. It was hard to say who was the more pleased, Bill or ourselves. He was enrolled at Robert Gordon's College, an excellent institution academically, but one which suffered in his eyes from the crushing disadvantage of playing rugby union football. We promised to do what we could in the way of arranging games for the summer.

A few weeks later, Mrs Edgar, our neighbour directly across the stair from us in Deanston Drive, welcomed her elder son home from the Merchant Navy on extended leave. He had brought with him a hand of bananas and with great generosity she sent a dozen or so across the closemouth. We boys enjoyed bananas and of course remembered them but Julie was scared stiff by their shape and did not want anything to do with them. We therefore ate hers to spare her any further distress. Indeed we did more, we went across to congratulate Mrs Edgar on the safe return of her son and received yet another banana each. We might even have gone back again to enquire after his continued welfare but my mother got to know about it and threatened us with disembowelling if we set foot on the Edgar doormat again.

American phrases began to creep into everyday life and strange new words such as *Jeep* and *GIs* became common currency. Two neighbouring boys, George McDevitt and John McDougall, took to wandering the lane at the back of the house with arms linked, tunelessly whistling *Anchors Aweigh*. I think this choice of song was linked, however inappropriately, to Warship Week, one of the huge fund-raising exercises for the Services which were held from time to time. These were held for each Service in turn, Wings For Victory and Salute the Soldier being the equivalents of Warship Week, and Glaswegians were always told how much Birmingham had subscribed and were exhorted by their Lord Provost to do better. The purpose was as much as anything to mop up some of the surplus money that was floating around. Almost everyone was in work by this time, wages were high and there was very little to spend them on. The civilian population had, therefore, to be encouraged to sub-scribe directly to the war effort. A fighter plane could be put in the air for £5,000, a bomber came much dearer at five times that sum. Lady MacRobert was held up to us as a shining example. She had lost several of her sons on service with the Royal Air Force and from her own personal fortune had provided aircraft which would be flown by the young pilots who were being trained to take the place of her own boys. New aircraft were coming on the scene now, Typhoons, Mosquitoes, Beaufighters, Liberators were joining the classic planes of the war, the Spitfires, Swordfish, Hurricanes, Blenheims and Halifaxes.

At street corners and in the public parks, meetings continued to be held calling for the creation of a Second Front and it was clear that this could not long be delayed. There was an unexpressed but definite belief that we must do more for the Russians than we had yet managed. Swords of Stalingrad, and Red Cross football inter-nationals for them, however well-intentioned and graced by the highest patronage, that of Mrs Churchill, were scarcely enough. There was a real pro-Russian feeling by this time and the names of their generals, Budyenny, Voroshilov, Zhukov and Timoshenko

were as well known as those of film stars or international footballers. My father insisted that the great Timoshenko was really an
Irishman in exile but we did not believe him as we would have done
three years earlier.

Finally, in June, the invasion was launched amid great anxiety.
We had heard and read about Hitler's Fortress Europe and could
understand something of the difficulty in getting masses of men and
material ashore. The first few days were very worrying indeed—
would this turn out to be merely another Dieppe on a larger scale?
Then it became clear that the troops had established a firm footing
and were in the process of breaking out from the beachheads. When
we broke up for the summer holidays, there were more Allied troops
in Europe than there had been in 1939 and much more was
happening.

By now there had been a real combing-out of manpower. Women
had been conscripted, were in the Services in large numbers and
were doing jobs hitherto reserved exclusively for men, such as
driving tramcars. We thought we saw our conductress of the gloves
and the rose at the helm of one of the new tramcars but we were not
quite sure. The "new" trams had been introduced just after the
Coronation in 1937 and would remain the "new" trams until they
were taken out of service a quarter of a century later.

Nowhere was the shortage of manpower becoming more
apparent than in the schools. By now all the able-bodied male
teachers had gone, except the occasional science man who was also
doing some war work in the evenings. Music was a subject which I
liked very well and up till now at Holyrood my teacher had been the
redoubtable Nora Gilfillan. She wore her grey hair very short and it
was iodine yellow at the fringes. Nora had a deep contralto voice
and was determined to improve our vowel sounds, being firm in the
opinion that the Glasgow "u" was the ugliest sound on God's earth,
an opinion in which she may well have been correct. We did
exercises which were designed to change our "grew" sound into
"igloo" and chanted dutifully "Oxo cubes are good for the 'floo".
In her choice of songs she was eminently sensible and she kept the
boys at such things as *Shenandoah* and *A Hundred Pipers* until we
were in the fourth year when the classes were mixed and the girls
could exercise a restraining influence on us.

About then, she became seriously ill and to take her place an old
man, Mr Dorman, came out of retirement. He was a frail, gentle-
manly soul who played the 'cello. We christened him Felix and gave

him a hell of a time. His choice of songs was ludicrously inapt for the collection of young Philistines sent his way by a severe fate. The first song he attempted to teach us pointed the road to disaster, although the subject, the outlaw Robin Hood, might have seemed sufficiently promising.

Let's seek the bower of Robin Hood for 'tis his wedding day,
And merrily in blithe Sherwood young men and maidens play.

If this was bad it was as nothing to the follow-up, *The Bailiff's Daughter of Islington*. This was in any event scarcely guaranteed to strike a responsive chord in Glaswegian breasts but it contains a singularly unfortunate line: "A penny, kind sir, just a penny," she said, "will relieve me of much pain". This was too much for the class bully, Joe "Bull" Connelly, who lay full length along the bench of the Lecture Room and when we reached the line quoted above, would give a moan of simulated anguish, out of sight of old Felix who continued to saw dreamily on his 'cello. In later years "Bull" Connelly became a perfectly likeable lad but it was asking too much of flesh and blood to let such songs pass without ribald comment. We were very glad when Nora Gilfillan reappeared and if we were glad, Felix Dorman's reaction can be well imagined.

So we went back to Kirn and by this time it would almost have been possible to walk from Kirn across the Firth to Gourock on the decks of the dozens of ships that lay at the Tail of the Bank. Great liners, capital warships and submarines, together with aircraft carriers were strewn so thickly on the river as almost to become invisible after a day or so. Bill had come down from Aberdeen and Alan Irons was back from Hamilton. We played golf with the practised skill of old hands and already I had decided that I was never going to stand comparison with Alan on any golf course.

I could however do something which he could not and that was win Go As You Please competitions. In our financial calculations my winning of the competition was regarded as a banker. I pondered over my choice of piece and decided to enter during the second week of our month's stay. On two afternoons I visited the Castle Gardens and noticed an interesting variation in the rules from the year before. There was now no age limit: children and adults were lumped in together. What should I play, I wondered? *In a Persian Market* by Alfred Ketelby was on my short list, good descriptive stuff, with *The Arrival of the Princess, The Caravan Prepares to Depart and the Jugglers in the Market Place*, all giving the audience something to get hold of, something to which they could relate. Perhaps I might even write a short introduction in which I would craftily include a few verbal signposts.

I finally decided that this would be to sell my public short. They deserved to be educated, to be moved up-market. I would perform for them the first movement of the Beethoven *Piano Sonata Op 27 No 2*, the *Moonlight*. There were one or two difficulties posed by this choice. The first was that unless the acoustics are particularly good, it is a difficult piece of music to hear, since it rarely if ever rises above *mezzoforte*. The second was that I was nowhere near well-equipped enough technically to attempt it although it could be argued that the first difficulty might well cancel out the second. It was enough—I had chosen.

There could have been very few more astounding tributes to the tolerance of the British people during the war than the fact that I won my heat. Coming off the stage I was quite composed, affecting not to hear the murmurs of "That's the wee fellow who won it here last year . . . *very* good he was". I hadn't even required family or friends to come along at this stage. I would reserve their support for the Friday final when it mattered. My line to them was that it had been rather a bore to forego the afternoon round of golf but that to help out our financial position it was a sacrifice that I was perfectly prepared to make.

Friday came and I set off for the Castle Gardens with my retinue. I was drawn to go fourth and knew that none of the first three turns provided any reason for being anxious. I came on, played comparatively well in a piece in which I was out of my depth and had there been a clapometer or other measurement of audience applause, I was certainly home and dry. Then I noticed a fine-featured, well-built young man walking on to the stage in company with my friend, the Colonel Sanders-like manager of the concert hall and gardens complex. I wondered sourly for a second why this young fellow was not in Normandy killing Germans instead of attempting to take the money from me. Then, as the manager carefully lined him up in front of the microphone, I realised why he was not. He was blind.

As it happened, he had a very pleasant voice, though his delivery was rough and untutored. He was in fact in the great tradition of the "singing bunnet", the little Glasgow man who will always give tongue in a Glasgow pub at a certain stage of the evening. My rival was not a little man but a fine-looking young fellow and he was not my rival because there was no contest. From his first lines — "My

116

deevoshun, is endless and deep as the oshun" — there could be only one outcome. He finished to a storm of applause and the three contestants after him were equally wasting their time. I came second and the Colonel Sanders man gave me two shillings from his own pocket so that there was very little in it financially but artistically I was shattered. How could they prefer *My Deevoshun* to the *Moonlight*?

Being older, we were now allowed to roam comparatively freely, even to the extent of voyaging on the *Lucy Ashton* across to Helensburgh to visit the baths there. The Helensburgh baths were no great shakes, being open-air and Siberian, but the travelling was all. Even at that period of the war there was still a tearoom of sorts on the steamer and it was possible to get right up to the bows and watch the water parting cleanly only three or four feet below eye-level. The tea-room was a great attraction and even at this late short-commons stage of the war could usually provide some teabread in the shape of coffee buns, Paris buns and plain cookies. I devised the notion, my brothers following more reluctantly, of having a "oner" competition, the idea being to swallow one or more of the aforementioned teabread at a single go. It could be done and was done, although the diameter of the buns, it has to be said, had shrunk somewhat from their lavish pre-1939 dimensions. We must have been a less than pleasing aesthetic sight to those who had the misfortune to be our fellow passengers.

This was the year when Phil's aristocratic upbringing got the better of him. There was a little steam yacht round in the Holy Loch which had been commandeered for Admiralty work and Phil told Alan that this had been our family yacht before the war and that my father had very decently relinquished it when the call came. I don't think he convinced Alan for a moment but by the end of the holiday he had done a very fair job on himself.

Alan went back to Hamilton, Bill to Aberdeen and we to Glasgow but before winter settled in there were one or two other changes of scene. My father paid almost his first visit to Ireland since he had taken us over in 1939 and Julie went with him. My mother looked after the *Ailsa Craig* and it was decided that my grandmother should take over the Shawlands house and Kathleen while we went to stay in Cowie Street. This arrangement had considerable advantages because clearly my mother was going to be far too busy downstairs in the shop to keep any very close eye on us.

We exploited the situation to the full. Being given money for the local Kinning Park pictures, we walked instead to Eglinton Street and there in the Coliseum we saw the first film of a most marvellous young comedian. The verbal dexterity of Danny Kaye knocked us over completely and for weeks we hurled his tongue-wrenching, gat-giddle *Mailman's Song* from his film *Up In Arms* at each other. We regarded this as a great breach in the wall of protocol: we had been on our own to "the town pictures" and henceforth could cite it as a precedent.

I could also henceforth use Dinah Shore as the yardstick against which I measured any female band singer. She had the melancholy experience of watching far less gifted but more conventionally good-looking young women being chosen for roles for which her innate musicianship made her the ideal choice.

Vaulting ambition unseated us only three days later. We set off on Saturday afternoon to attend the Glasgow Cup Final at Hampden Park between Rangers and Celtic but this was a match in which we had not the slightest proprietary interest and I had formulated an alternative plan. We would go to watch Queen's Park . . . *at Dumbarton!* Into Queen Street Station we strolled with the finesse of old city hands, went downstairs to the Low Level platform and boarded the Dumbarton train. We found the ground easily and enjoyed the game, the more so that Queen's got a creditable 2-2 draw. We had been to a match out of Glasgow!

We must have been over-elated on our return because our mother was on to us at once. Her technique was disarmingly simple. She asked us what the score had been at Hampden and who the scorers were. We gave these answers without hesitation, having been careful to ascertain them from returning Hampden spectators in the station. She then asked artlessly which way Rangers had kicked in the first half. My "The King's Park end" beat Frankie's "Towards the Mount" and Philip's honest "Don't know" by a tenth of a second. We got a tremendous dressing-down and a promise of physical punishment when our father returned from Ireland. We pointed out that in very sooth we would have been in much more danger at a Rangers-Celtic game but that availed us nothing and the evening ended in fraternal recriminations, "Don't know" indeed!

Something my father brought back from Ireland provided the means by which I worked my passage back to society. It was a decorated floral half tea-set, still available in the Irish Free State when all in Britain were plain white. It so happened that within a day or two of the arrival of the china, much-admired by passing neighbours, a sister, I think Kathleen, accidentally knocked a cup from the living-room table but I averted disaster with a slip fielder's catch inches from the floor.

Towards the end of September a marvellous thing happened. It was decided that the risk of air raids had dwindled to the point where it would be possible to reintroduce street lighting which would be of almost peacetime standards of brilliance. There would be no decorative lighting and certainly no neon signs but when the lights were switched on the effect was astonishing. The entire population of Glasgow rushed out into the streets and many read newspapers under the lamps, as if trying to prove a point. For several nights afterwards together with our friends, we climbed to a deserted tennis court in High Camphill and from this plateau in the middle of the woods there was a wonderful view of the city hung once more with lights. It was most moving, and the notion came to me that this must have been something like what the evangelist was trying to convey when, in writing of the temptations of Christ, he describes the Devil's taking Him up to a mountaintop below which the cities of the world were laid out before Him.

We were very fortunate that such a restoration was possible because shortly before there had been a resumption of air raids on the south of England, this time by the even more frightening pilotless aircraft, the V1's. So it came about that Scotland and England were singing different songs of the blitz. It was still appropriate down there to sing *Mr Brown from London Town* and *London Pride*. I remember marvelling that on the same subject two songs of such varying quality could be written. *Mr Brown from London Town* dealt in relentless jollity:

Mr Brown from London Town, had a job to do,
Meant to see it through, and he did it too.
Mr Brown from London Town sent the wife away,
Sent the kids to play, miles and miles away.
Things blew up and things blew down, seemed a bloomin' shame.
Bloomin' fire and flames, Blimey! what a game.
But who stood up and saved the town when London Bridge was
    falling down?
Mr Brown from London Town, Oi! Mr Brown.

Compared with that, Noel Coward's *London Pride* was all elegance and whipcord grace:

Every blitz your resistance toughening,

> From the Ritz to the Anchor and Crown
> Nothing ever could quite replace
> The grace of London Town.

It was still hard in Southern England and would get harder. We, in contrast, could indulge ourselves in the more sentimental songs and soft lays of peace:

> When they sound the last all-clear
> How happy my darling we'll be,
> When they turn on the lights
> And the dark lonely nights
> Are only a memory.

and the song that everybody had sung on the night the black-out had been lifted:

> When the lights go on again, all over the world,
> And the boys are home again, all over the world,
> Then there'll be time for things like wedding rings
> And free hearts will sing,
> When the lights go on again, all over the world.

The renewed bombing of London was a sign that there was still some way to go. As I delivered my morning papers I read that the Guards' Chapel had received a direct hit during a service and that a flying bomb had narrowly missed Lord's while a match was in progress. I regret to say that the second item affected me more than the first. There was another evacuation of schoolchildren in progress. We could vouch for that because, even at this late stage of the conflict, a few London children were arriving at Holyrood to swell the ranks.

So the war was not over but the Allies had Rome and they had Paris and there was no doubt now what the eventual outcome would be. The question was, *when?*, not *what?* The taking of Paris revived interest in a 1940 song, because strangely there seemed to be no number written to celebrate the freeing of the city. The song that re-emerged was therefore one associated with capitulation and the defeat of 1940.

> The last time I saw Paris, her heart was young and gay,
> No matter how they change her, I'll remember her that way.

When the harvest holidays came Frank went off with the school to Perth and triumphantly stayed the course as his elder brother had not managed to do the year before. I thought I had the better part in

120

going to see my first serious play, James Bridie's *Mr Bolfry*. I quite enjoyed the theological discussion which formed much of the argument of the play and thought the very last scene, when the umbrella of Mr Bolfry (in reality His Satanic Majesty) danced off the stage under its own steam to be a triumph of stagecraft. I knew that this was something which I would instinctively prefer to films where there was no contact between performer and audience.

As the King had said in one of his first wartime broadcasts: "But westward look, the land is bright". The Home Guard now stood down, all threat of invasion over. Middle-aged and elderly men, they had kept thankless watch and ward and kept dozens of comedians in work. Through it all they had served uncomplainingly and met these heavy additional demands for, of course, each of them was doing a normal job, not infrequently in an office or factory which had been denuded of its young men. Now they marched off-stage a little ponderously but with justifiable pride, perhaps their greatest value lying in the fact that they had never been required in any large-scale action. The West of Scotland had by this time gone for a whole calendar year without an air raid and there was talk of extra food being issued with the Christmas rations.

In all this, we were thinking of and concentrating on Europe. To defeat Germany and Italy would not necessarily be to defeat Japan, and one of the things I also picked up from the newspapers was that 16-year-olds would be registering for service early in the New Year. Things were getting just a bit close for me if the war had even two years more to run.

Exotic visitors flitted in and out of Glasgow. De Gaulle and Sikorski, the Polish general, I saw, but this did not make up for missing Joe Louis, the world heavyweight champion, whose flying visit had unfortunately taken place while we were at Kirn. Parties of Russian trade unionists were towed round factories to encourage the workers and a Russian Cossack troupe performed at the Glasgow Fair carnival on Glasgow Green. Inevitably though, the great influence was the American, and our radio reflected the United States way of life and viewpoint as never before. This was done not only with American dance music or "swing" as the current term was. We enjoyed the music of Benny Goodman, Guy Lombardo, Xavier Cugat, Tommy Dorsey, Harry James and above all Glenn Miller, but it was not only through music that the American troops and ourselves were reminded and informed of

121

events back home. On Sunday mornings commentaries on National League ice hockey were broadcast and we dashed back from church to hear of the doings of the Detroit Redwings, the Boston Bruins, the Toronto Maple Leafs and the Montreal Canadians. The strident voice of the broadcaster on the opening — He shoots! He scores! And the game is over! — was our introduction to a more raucous form of sports commentating. Then in the afternoon the contest was more sedate with *Transatlantic Call - People to People* and, later, *Transatlantic Quiz*.

There was a strong sense of things moving, things happening. Just before Christmas Cissie Foxworthy took us to see our first French film made in wartime and, so the buzz had it, "smuggled out of France". We trooped expectantly into the Cosmo cinema in Rose Street looking to view some stirring tale of the Resistance. We were well up in the doings of the Maquis, indeed Pat Harrigan and I had begun a few months before to write a very convoluted play about four British airmen shot down over France who were trying to escape with the help of the Resistance. With a flash of inspiration we called this play *Escape*. It soon got bogged down in all sorts of complications as in order to facilitate the escape Alf, Dave, Joe and Nigel (the pilot and therefore Nigel) had to become Jacques, Gautier, Didi and Armand. We soon could not remember which one was which and in a short space of time could not muster the enthusiasm to care. The project fell apart in feeble bickering.

If not about the Resistance I imagined that this film might concern itself with Vichy France against the Free French, the former being those who followed the official line that after 1940 the Government of France had vested in Marshal Pétain and the unattractive Pierre Laval, and the Free French, those who had followed De Gaulle since the summer of that year. The two sides had reached a situation of civil war in Syria in 1941 and again in certain areas of North Africa.

The film that we saw, *Nous les Gosses* (Us Kids) concerned itself with neither subject and indeed did not mention the war from start to finish. It told of a group of schoolboys who in the course of playing football in the school playground accidentally break an ornate and expensive window in one of the school buildings. The story then dealt with the attempts of the boys to raise money for a replacement window. We enjoyed the film thoroughly. It had a refreshing realism which we would not have found in a British film of the time, and we could certainly sympathise with the predicament in which the French pupils found themselves. We wondered greatly, however, why this film should have had to be smuggled out of France and decided that it must have everything to do with the thoroughness of the Gestapo.

I was half afraid that I would be called into action against the Gestapo and half afraid that I would not. This fear of not being called upon had nothing to do with the "I hope the show doesn't finish before we get there, chaps" of First World War mythology. It had its roots in the fear that I might be smaller than the Forces would need or want. I might have made the school team but no amount of wishing could mask the fact that I was still comparatively tiny. I could have served as the original for the small boy in the cartoon who on applying to join the Guards was told by a kindly sergeant, "We'll be delighted to have you, lad, if in the next fortnight you can pass the aptitude test and grow three feet."

I was not concerned with the Guards but with the school cadet corps. I was of age to join but was determined that I would not do so until I sprouted at least a little. The nominal command of the cadets was exercised by the Headmaster, who for this purpose bore the title of Major Francis Graham. Nor was it unearned as he had been commissioned and decorated in the 1914-18 war, which earned him our reluctant respect when we got to hear of it. The day-to-day work of the platoon was carried out by the saturnine Maths and Classics master, Bob "Nick" Carter. He was tall, sallow, wore glasses and could have passed for Lulu's brother. I had never met anyone then who had a more imposing presence. He seemed to us like a very tall and rather good-looking Japanese. My terror of him (misplaced for he was the kindest of men) went back to First Year when he had taken us for Latin. The room where we met was at the end of a long verandah, a good 80 yards from the staffroom. Often on a Thursday afternoon, when change-over rang and he would be a little late, we sat there, hope mounting by the second that he was absent. Then, in the distance, the swing doors would crash open and Nick, gown billowing behind him, would come stalking along the corridor. Our babble died away dispiritedly with his springy walk, ceasing completely as he pulled open the door and in his Preston accent drawled, "Take out your Civis Romaanus!"

I had less cause to fear than most, being comparatively facile in the language at that early stage but he struck terror into me as no teacher before or since. And yet there was nothing to fear. He was the kindest and most ill-fated of men and he would die within two years. His discovery that there were two people in the school who cared about cricket eventually led to the forming of a bond between us, not that I could look to that to save me if I stumbled while translating the harrowing tale of Mucius Scaevola.

He brought the same standards of hard work and neatness to the cadets that he did to the classroom and he had a very good sergeant in a classmate of mine, John Fildes, one of those who had been evacuated from England at an earlier period. Pat Harrigan had joined the Air Training Corps and looked very fetching in his uniform but then Pat was well beyond six feet. My Uncle Joe, who had joined the navy and had by now been posted abroad, understood my agonies and wrote very helpful letters from Freetown in Sierra Leone, where the fortunes of war had sent him. The censor had been busy on his letters but he seemed to be enjoying life and in no very great hurry for the war to finish.

I did what I could, which was not very much. I tore up the tenement flights every day as I distributed the newspapers. I stretched in bed at night as I read of the adventures of Rockfist Rogan, RAF. I could only read of these fortnightly now since restrictions on paper meant that the *Champion*, Rockfist's home paper, only appeared with half its previous frequency. Rockfist was an amiable member of the RAF who spent the war on dangerous and secret missions to Europe, normally France. Having carried out his orders totally successfully, Rockfist felt free to pop into the local town hall where there was a boxing tournament in progress. He would enter the ring under some assumed name—French promoters seemed to show a one hundred per cent willingness to change their bill at the last moment—and take on the local or national champion. I seem to remember that on occasions the latter, puzzled, would say something on the lines of "Didn't I see you at the Berlin Olympics of 1936?" whereat Rockfist would smile and, delivering a left jab and a right cross, dance nimbly out of reach. Sometimes he varied the procedure by employing his leisure moments to duff up the chief of the local Gestapo who was invariably a swinish person well in line for a beating.

I stretched in bed in the mornings. I visited the gym at lunchtime when I didn't have to and hung manfully from wallbars and beams. When dispatched by my father for cigarettes, I ran with giant strides round many shops, for even in the darkest days of the war my father was a stickler where tobacco was concerned. "No Prize Crop or Pasha!" was his invariable cry and woe betide the child who brought either back for want of something better. He was the mildest of men but to introduce either brand to 207 was to incur his high displeasure.

His contempt for the strong and exotic, not to say bizarre, Pasha was particularly marked. "They affect your next of kin," he would say. My mother, a dedicated anti-smoker would occasionally suggest that Daniel might give them up for the war but my father had few pleasures and very properly refused, not that it was a serious expectation on my mother's part. Yet she, like me, genuinely believed that smoking stunted your growth and no amount of cigarette-puffing six-foot Hollywood stars would induce her to believe otherwise.

All the small men I knew were comedians, such as Arthur Askey or Lou Costello, excellent at making people laugh and no doubt devoted husbands and fathers but I wanted more altitude. Small men could play association football and some such as Jimmy Mason of Third Lanark did so very well, but they were inside-forwards and I was fully aware that I lacked that kind of dexterity. So, I got on with it and "got stuck in" at school, at least in those subjects which I liked. My father had bought for the three boys a fine set of encyclopaedias called *The Wonder Books*. They were beautifully illustrated and stoutly bound, and their price of eight guineas was much more than the average weekly wage of the time. I devoured them from Volume 1 to Volume 8 and I think I understood most of what I read. I therefore flourished in the liberal arts subjects and "still they gazed and still the wonder grew". It was a pity that nothing else did.

Chapter Eight

1945:
The fire will dwindle into glowing embers

ONE of the oddest things about wars is the suddenness with which they finish. In September 1918 the end of the Great War had seemed far off and while no doubt the American South was doomed at the start of 1865, few would have thought that Northern troops would be in Richmond within four months.

So it proved with us in 1945. As the New Year dawned there seemed plenty of fight left in the Germans. They had counter-attacked successfully in the Ardennes on the Franco-Belgian border and were reputed to have caused great consternation by their use of English-speaking troops who had spent time in the United States as young men. These soldiers passed themselves off as genuine Americans and had to be detected by Intelligence questioning on who had won the World Series the previous autumn. This aspect of things was no doubt overplayed. It seemed very likely that German soldiers in such a situation would have taken great care to find out the World Series results, but the Americans did take a battering for a couple of weeks, and one of their leaders, General McAuliffe, found himself among those whose wartime sayings became memorable when he refused the German demand to surrender the town of Bastogne with a curt "Nuts!".

The failure of the Arnhem initiative had meant that the hope of a finish by Christmas 1944 would go unrealised and that the Dutch would pass another winter under Nazi occupation. But the counter-attack in the Ardennes peaked and spent itself and it was, this time, to be the Third Reich's last throw in the west. Seven hundred miles to the east the Germans were in full retreat with "the Russians in their wake" as Dark Satanic Mills had so percipiently put it in the class magazine of 1943. Germany was being compressed relentlessly in a vice and was now being bombed around the clock.

The war was going well and in our own little corner of the tight

126

little island we were in high glee. Our football team, Queen's Park, had risen to unimagined heights of creativity and success. On the first two days of the year we watched them beat Third Lanark and Rangers and indeed they would not taste of defeat until Easter Monday when they lost to Celtic at Parkhead. Having established our right at home to become travelling supporters we followed them around the West of Scotland, bumping out to Coatbridge by tram-car in a snowstorm to watch them triumph and turning back up the terracings at Airdrie just in time to see the third and tying goal which preserved their unbeaten record.

The war was good for Queen's Park since the absence of full-time professional football as a permissible occupation meant that the good players might as well stay at Hampden for the time being and they did. Our goalkeeper was the blond matinee idol Bobby Brown, lithe and brave, our right-winger was a Maths lecturer at Glasgow University and later at St Andrews, Lindsay Hodge, and the left-half and captain was Doctor Alec Cross, a magnificent terrier of a wing-half who tackled with a fair ferocity that belied his five foot seven inches. We used to think that he played as hard as he did in order to ensure some custom for his surgery. Spring brought this glorious surge to a close as in addition to the defeat by Celtic, Rangers also proved too strong in the semi-final of the League Cup. The signs of peace were in evidence on the football field. Kilmarnock were not quite back in full business but were fielding a reserve side and one or two of the vanished junior clubs such as St Roch's had made a very welcome reappearance.

Goal average and pointage I could calculate in the turn of an eye, scores and scorers I could rhyme off unthinkingly but there my mathematical aptitude or indeed adequacy ended. I memorised the long proof of Pythagoras' Theorem without comprehending a syllable of it, and when it came to Deductions I painstakingly wrote, Given, Required To Prove, Construction, Proof and then moodily chewed my pencil. I had still two years to do at school after the current session but was well on my way to setting up my melancholy record of never working out a single geometrical deduction in my life. "Nick" Carter who now took us for Mathematics rather than Latin hauled me out to the board one day to demonstrate some tedious nonsense about the angle between the chord and the tangent being equal to that in the alternate segment. I cared nothing if it was or not, and I particularly did not want to be taken out to the board because I was wearing my first pair of long trousers and rather peculiar they were, being US Navy in cut and with pearl buttons on the hip pockets and side pockets. They were US Navy in cut because they originated with the US Navy although how they had got my length is now unclear. They were only approximately my length in any event and "Nick" felt moved to comment to the rest of the class, "Oh, look, young Robert's got his long trousers on", which did nothing for my attempts to prove the wretched proposition.

We made various artistic excursions from school. On several occasions we went to the Dixon Halls in Crosshill where a detachment of the Scottish Orchestra, as it then was, gave concerts to parties of school children. It can hardly have been the most exhilarating of assignments for the musicians and some of them only too clearly regarded it as punishment drill. Above the susurration of the audience such pieces as *Morning* from Grieg's *Peer Gynt* suite struggled to be heard but the last movement of the *William Tell Overture*, as yet unlinked to the Lone Ranger, could be relied on to provide a rousing finale. I was surprised to see the English principal, Tommy Stairs, reading a book in the middle of such glorious sound, for even at half strength, and with the orchestra sometimes playing sloppily, I found the music marvellous.

The conductor was a small, dark, neatly bearded man called Warwick Braithwaite but there were two other members of the orchestra who interested us rather more. The orchestra ranks had of course been sadly depleted of male players by the war and the leader was a dark, good-looking lady called Jean Rennie who had excellent legs which she crossed and re-crossed with gratifying frequency on the elevated platform. The other musician who took our eye was the harpist who wore a wig of startling improbability. Before the concert proper began, various members of the orchestra would demonstrate their instruments for us and after giving us a few *glissandi* the harpist would invariably finish his spot by saying, "And of course all harpists hope to get to heaven", which was better the first time than it became with repetition.

Glasgow schools had an excellent tradition of interesting their children in the theatre. It had started well before the war when we had been taken to see Bertha Waddell's Children's Theatre where after every scene the presenter would return to the stage and say, "Item number . . .", at which the audience would chorus SEEEEVEN or whichever number was appropriate. Bertha Waddell had been strong on fairy tales with heroes looking for magic axes or losing things:

I have lost my golden dragon-fly,
Won't you help me find it, Chee Su-Li?

Now, in the closing months of the war, we were to make the aquaintance of the Bard through the school. I had already done this by going to see the Laurence Olivier-Ralph Richardson season with the Old Vic company but nevertheless I enjoyed Donald Wolfit in *Hamlet*, although we found his curtain speech very irritating as he clutched the drapes to him in an apparent state of total exhaustion. We loved the way he dealt with the problem of a large cast-list for a small cast by such devices as a shout of "Stand fast, and pass the word along" as the fourth soldier of the Danish or Polish or Norwegian or Scottish army entered from the wings. The effect was to give the impression of a mighty host champing at the bit in the wings. It reminded one of the fictitious production of *Ali Baba* at the Queen's Theatre in Glasgow where the hero was reputed to have instructed his band of thieves by merry shout to the wings, "You two come with me, the other thirty-eight wait outside".

School was beginning to gear itself for the return to peace. Planning became long-term rather than week to week. When I had arrived, just over three years before, part of the school had still been occupied by young Polish soldiers who enlivened our days with their antics, notably on the day when they removed surreptitiously the engine of the car which belonged to a popular technical teacher, "Beery" Hunter. The Poles had long since gone and many of the young boys were dead, in North Africa, Sicily and at Monte Cassino. One of them would come back to teach in the early 1960s in Holyrood and in 1962 return to Poland for the first time in 23 years to see his mother again.

There was another death too, that of Pat Harrigan's elder brother, Major Jim Harrigan, who was killed about the time of the Rhine crossing. He was a good bit older than Pat and inevitably they had not seen a great deal of each other over the last five years or so but to be cut down so near to what was now clearly final victory did seem to be particularly cruel. It was yet another reminder to us of how lucky we had been in our own family circumstances that we had had no one at risk over the last six years.

A death marked the last great sporting event of the war, the international of April 1945, against England. We were in an even keener state of anticipation for this match than usual because in the Scotland side, for the first time since 1933, appeared not one Queen's Park player but two. Bobby Brown was in goal and J R

("Tony") Harris had been called in at centre-forward at the last minute. As we made ready to go to the match that morning we heard that the President of the United States of America, Franklin Delano Roosevelt, had died suddenly. This was a great shock since FDR was infinitely better known to the British public than any previous President and he had cropped up constantly in song. Judy Garland had trilled

> I'm mad about good books, can't get my fill,
> And Franklin Roosevelt's looks, give me a thrill.

while a Nazi blitz on London had brought about a practical expression of sympathy from the President that led to the writing of *Thanks, Mr Roosevelt*.

He had been seen constantly in newsreels and heard on radio in his famous *Fireside Chats*. Now he was dead and nothing was known about his successor, Vice-President Harry Truman. In pouring rain, the vast Hampden crowd stood in a, for once, unbroken silence for him as the national anthems were played. It was a melancholy afternoon altogether. A Scottish player was injured in collision with England goalkeeper Frank Swift after only 30 seconds and had to be taken off, although as a special act of grace the Scots were permitted to field a substitute. The powerful English side tore the home side apart and not even the presence of two Queen's Parkers could stem the tide. We even contrived to miss a penalty kick and the purgatorial afternoon ended with England having scored six goals to our one.

Just before the winter ended I had once more outreached myself musically by applying to BBC Scotland *Children's Hour* for an audition. I don't think I knew why I did this even at the time, certainly not in the form of a piano audition where the competition was fearful. I was sure that some day I wanted to broadcast and this was all that I could think of to offer. I dragged my mother off by tramcar through a cold March evening to Queen Margaret Drive in Glasgow where I was shown into the studio and a disembodied voice asked me kindly what I proposed to play. When I told it that I would like to play Chopin's *Minute Waltz*, the voice, prophetically, murmured, "A very interesting choice".

It may have been interesting but hardly successful. I was inclined to think that a successful performance of this work was one which trimmed the European record to 58 seconds and there was no chance that my abysmal technique could support this. At the end of a minute of slurred, scamped, snatched sound, the voice with quite undeserved kindness said, "Thank you very much, Robert. I don't think you are quite ready for us yet". Not this side of the grave I wasn't and what should have been said was, "How dare you presume to waste our time, you untalented pipsqueak?" As it was, on the way home, instead of apologising to my mother for having put her to a totally unnecessary and physically painful ordeal, I chattered on about the deficiencies of the instrument and how I had not been allowed to warm my hands before beginning to play, as if either of these things could have made any conceivable difference. When I continued in the same vein after reaching home, my father shut me up with an unwonted savagery and promptness.

Then, so quickly it scarcely seemed to be happening at all, it was all over. Terrified by the Russian onslaught in the East, from which horror stories were already beginning to emerge, the Germans stampeded to surrender to Americans, British or French in the West. Resistance in Italy collapsed and Mussolini and his mistress, Clara Petrucci, were hanged by partisans, with venom, without dignity. In death as in life, perhaps the *Beano* had been right — "Musso da Wop, he's a big-a-da-flop".

For perhaps a week we lived in the daily expectation that it was all officially over and the wireless had to contradict this, saying sternly that no cease-fire had as yet been signed and reminding us that the war had still to be prosecuted. We heard that Hitler and his bride of a few hours, Eva Braun, had committed suicide as the Russians entered the eastern suburbs of Berlin, in a reach-me-down pastiche of Wagnerian opera. Then at last it was official.

On the morning when we knew that the war in Europe was over a flag was hoisted over the school bearing the inscription "Cave Canem" (beware of the dog). We thought this a great joke, an opinion not shared by the Dog, the Headmaster, who made earnest attempts to track down the imaginative and classical culprits. Nobody was disposed to take the inquest very seriously or to offer him any real assistance. Much more typical of the day was the revelation that the fearsome Nora Gilfillan was a very fair honky-tonk pianist as from her room the chords of *Pinetop's Boogie* sounded down the well of the staircase and through the school.

We were given a holiday of course and in a spontaneous starburst of joy and relief, street parties were organised. Tables were dragged out into the middle of the road, covered with paper and tied or lashed together. Our piano was commandeered to my mother's not unmixed delight. Every house contributed sandwiches, vast teapots came out of retirement, impromptu groups played for dancing and of course the neighbouring children did turns and the adults sang. For the last time, the dreaded *March of the Indians* was "received with much acceptance" as local Scottish papers used curiously to say. My sisters danced the Polish Festival dance — or was it the Russian Festival dance? — and a boy in 203, Leslie King, who really could play well, performed a Chopin *Mazurka*. The adults rendered *We'll Gather Lilacs, Accent--uate the Positive* and, however inappropriately, *Lilli Marlene*, which by some strange collective process was felt to be undoubtedly the best song to have come out of the war and the fact that it had been written for the other side was neither here or there. These parties were to run for the rest of the summer and indeed beyond that, moving indoors by September as the occasion for them changed and they became Welcome Home parties for men who had been prisoners-of-war. Close-mouths would be hung with Union Jacks and any bunting that miraculously might have survived since the Coronation of 1937 and Welcome Home Bill, Alec, Jock, Stevie, would be chalked or pipe-clayed on paths and buildings. The thin, returned men would accept this three-day spotlight uncomplainingly before returning to that civilian obscurity in which they would live out the rest of their lives.

They would not be returning to the world of 1939. That was gone beyond recall. It would have been so in any case and the result of the General Election of 1945 made only a difference of speed. The ink was hardly dry on the cease-fire at Luneberg Heath when the electoral truce which since 1939 had prevented Conservatives contesting Labour-held seats and vice versa was declared to be at an end. The holding of a General Election posed grave problems since a large number of voters, male and female, were abroad with the services. It was decided that there should be a three-week delay between polling day and the declaration of the poll to take account of this.

I followed the campaign with great interest as I had never seen a General Election before. My employer, Archie Gardner, was a great *Daily Express* man and it never occurred to him, or to me, but that Mr Churchill would be returned with a large majority. I attended a few meetings and was appalled at the lack of policy offered by the Conservative candidate. It boiled down to "He (Churchill) saw us through the war, he'll see us through the peace" and I felt that this was to misjudge the mood of the meeting although I was still sure that Churchill would win.

Certainly the Commonwealth Party, led by Sir Richard Acland, would not win although it was attracting a lot of publicity. The Commonwealth candidate for the Pollok constituency in which we lived was called Voisey Youldon, a name which might do well enough in Malden or Epsom but which was doomed to disaster in the kingdom of the Red and White Fergies. Nor did I think the Anarchists deserved to win. I was a bit partial here, as the Anarchist candidate had been rude and obscene to me when I asked him at a street meeting whether he did not think the last two words of his slogan — "Government is for slaves, free men govern themselves, join the anarchist federation" — were not a contradiction in terms. The last two words he addressed to me had nothing to do with his slogan.

When the three weeks of waiting were up, the Labour Party had won an astonishing victory and readers of the *Daily Express* were thunderstruck. The Conservatives had been humiliated and after the first dazed expectations of a Soviet had not been realised, it became apparent that they had deserved abundantly to be humiliated. Their campaign had been an affront to the voters and had consisted of nothing more than carrying the Prime Minister around like some form of primitive ju-ju. The electorate, widely separated by distance, had wisely and emphatically given its opinion that it wouldn't do and that men and women who had been torn away from their families for up to six years had not suffered as they had suffered to be given more of the same.

The Government was now faced with a very severe problem which was quite simply to remind and keep reminding the nation that the war was only half-over. VE Day meant exactly that, Victory in Europe. It had to guard against the very understandable national tendency to let the shoulders go down in a sigh of relief. It was essential that the country should know that there were still men dying every day in Burma and the Pacific Islands and, even more important, that many of the soldiers now in Europe would be required for service against Japan. Two years was the best estimate that anyone was prepared to make on the length of the forthcoming campaign and, given the Japanese attitudes towards death and surrender, it was likely to be an affair of island-hopping in which our own casualties would be very heavy. Even the most fanatical Germans had at the end an element of self-preservation which the Japanese would lack. The newsreel shots of the concentration camps of Dachau and Belsen did much by their horror to stiffen resolve for what would have to be done in the Pacific. If there had been the least doubt of the necessity for going to war, that now tended to disappear. It was in this peculiar in-between state of affairs that we spent the last wartime summer.

Frank McNaughton had come back to the Clyde with the *Zamalek* and on one of his short leaves he noticed that the visiting Australian Air Force cricket team would be playing at Hamilton Crescent, Glasgow, and he invited us to join him. We had watched club cricket often at Titwood and Shawholm and we had spread our favours impartially between Clydesdale and Poloc but here was a chance to see some top-class Australian State players and perhaps even Test players in action. There were 8,000 of us shoe-horned into the compact little West of Scotland ground on a day that for weather was all that could have been wished. Lindsay Hassett, who had come over with Bradman's Test side of 1938 did not play, much to our disappointment, but Keith Miller did and so too the great wicket-keeper, D K Carmody. We yelled our heads off as the Scots excelled themselves in bowling out this very strong side for a paltry 149 but what a revelation it was to see the Aussies exert themselves as they realised that perhaps they had taken the opposition too cheaply and might be in danger of defeat. The whole side seemed effortlessly to move up about three gears and Scotland were bundled out for 90. Afterwards a short exhibition match was played in the course of which a Scot, J M Fleming, offered himself as sacrificial lamb to Keith Miller who hit the ball far and high and often out of the ground. It was joke bowling of course, but given our unsophisticated level of appreciation we thought it wonderful and, at least in my case, were smitten for life.

In our more simplistic moments we had imagined the war ending on a Thursday, a meal of pre-war standard appearing on the table by Friday and newspapers and comics restored to their normal size and frequency of issue by the Saturday. It was not remotely like that. The edging back to normality was to be an infinitely slow process and would not be completed until the coronation of Queen Elizabeth II almost exactly eight years later.

At Kirn there were a few tentative signs, like the first branches floating past the doors of the Ark. The boom which had controlled the entry to the river had been dismantled, and in consequence it was now possible to sail from the Upper Firth to Rothesay. As far as the Craigendoran service was concerned, the beautiful veteran, the incomparable *Lucy Ashton*, was given this additional chore to do while her more glamorous sisters refitted at Bowling, but for the following season. We had seen the *Jeannie Deans* at Bowling on a choir outing and had been most impressed when Nora Gilfillan told us that she remembered dancing on the decks of that very vessel to piped gramophone music before the war. The *Jeannie* would be back, the *Lucy* soldiered on. Among the aristocrats of the LMS fleet, the *Duchess of Argyll* had been released from troopship tender duties and now undertook the Rothesay sailing. It was a great joy to see the funnels in the old liveries after the drab battleship-grey of the war and to see also the lights on the ships at night, particularly beautiful when they surmounted the white paint of a hospital ship, of which there were many, bringing back the prisoners of war from the camps all over Europe.

We stayed in a rather strange house, Woodside, next to Kirn Pier, with a rather weird landlady, Mrs Reid, who operated the curious Clyde coast system of "with attendance". This meant that the holidaymakers provided their own food but that this was prepared and cooked by the landlady. Mrs Reid was like every sinister house-keeper in a Hollywood film but she took her title, Fanny by Gas-light, from a British film and the fact that her house was without electricity. Each evening she would murmur that she would have to retire to take her medicine which we suspected contained at least some alcoholic content. Phil was also certain that Mrs Reid was apropriating some of the food to her own purposes. We were not as sure, although we suspected it. One afternoon towards tea-time, Phil came in, opened the deep kitchen larder and exclaimed, laughing theatrically, "What are you doing in that cupboard, Mrs Reid?", only to almost die with fright when she stepped out and said, "I'm just in looking for eggs for the tea".

The utility buses were given a very little petrol for a few bus runs and once again the chalked boards proclaimed the delights of Puck's Glen, Benmore, Cot House and Inveraray. We went on the last-named excursion and were greatly interested when passing along Loch Eck to see the monument set up to Captain John Lauder, son of Sir Harry and killed in the First World War.

My father managed a few days and enjoyed our company and also that of the family who were staying in the other half of the house. The star turn there was old Granny McIntyre who had as a girl worked in the Calico Dye Works in the Vale of Leven and remembered going to work bare-foot, with her feet wrapped in her petticoats in a vain attempt to keep them warm. She also remembered a winter which was so cold that for six weeks she had been able to skate on Loch Lomond without the least fear or danger.

Granny McIntyre was a vigorous user of the Scots tongue and she endorsed Philip's opinion of Mrs Reid as a caterer. Weak tea she could not abide, something she shared with my father. He referred to the landlady's tea as "workhouse tea" which he characterised as "one leaf floating upon the surface singing *Driven from home*". If in more charitable frame of mind he would elevate the brew to the status of "shamrock tea" but Granny McIntyre's unbending judgement was that "that wumman canny make tea. A' she can make is a pot o' wash."

For the last time too the mighty troopships swung at the Tail o' the Bank. We went over to Kilcreggan and boarded a motor-boat which took us out around the great vessels, engaged in transferring surplus American divisions to the Pacific. Our little boat bobbed and bounced under the tenement-like high sides of the massive transports. My father shouted up to the Yanks, "Keep an eye on Tojo, lads", and we were as foolishly and cravenly embarrassed for him as boys of that age are. The Americans waved back cheerfully and from their stance so high above us sent boxes of Hershey bars and chewing gum and crates of oranges hurtling towards our decks, any of which, had they registered a direct hit, might well have sunk us. Our skipper took cunning evasive action as the passengers retrieved the booty from the churning waters of the Clyde and somehow we worked out a reasonably equitable shareout of the Americans' bounty. The Americans went east to find themselves equally superfluous while back in Scotland, teams of Italian POWs played football matches against Scots sides in perfect amity and before long German teams would be doing the same, even with goalkeepers who wore Afrika Corps caps.

In mid-August I caught the mid-morning *Marchioness of Lorne* to go up to Glasgow to collect our meat rations. Food was still tight and we preferred to deal with our regular butcher, who tried, on a rota system, to give a little extra to each family from time to time. This was perfectly feasible since in almost every week there was some meat not taken up, but the shopkeeper had to be very careful that he did not fall foul of the officials of the Ministry of Food who gave the impression that they would have preferred to see the meat thrown away rather than that anyone should exceed his ration.

I had collected the meat and before returning to Kirn I had dropped in to see my grandmother in Cowie Street. As I came out of her house to return to the Central Station I noticed a great commotion in the streets and crowds of people surrounding a news-paper seller. I shouldered my way into the scrum and emerged with a paper. The Allies had dropped the first atomic bomb on Japan and, of course, shortly afterwards they dropped a second.

Try as I might, I cannot remember that there was any great indignation at this action by the Allies. The war had been ended abruptly; there would be no leapfrogging from island to island, winkling out pockets of fanatically brave Japanese troops. A great many British soldiers were going to live who might otherwise have died and in any case the Japanese were due not the slightest consideration after the manner in which they had behaved towards our civilian population in the Far East and to their prisoners-of-war. That was about the size of it, for certainly there was more vehement opposition to the bombing of such cities as Leipzig, Nuremburg and Dresden.

My other reaction was the only one there could have been, delighted relief. Another two years and it was very probable that my age group would have been involved. I was glad to have been spared and wished Pat Harrigan's brother had managed to hang on for another month. I had only ever seen him once and yet his death affected me because of the very randomness of it. The element of chance dealt its cards grotesquely even within the same family. Of two brothers who used to come about my grandfather's house before the war and who had joined up almost immediately, one had been through the Western Desert campaign, Sicily, and Anzio before being recalled to Britain for the invasion. It was from him that I learned that the D in D Day, which I had taken to mean Deliverance Day or Doom Day or something equally portentous, meant no more than the H in H Hour or the Y in Y Year. He went on to fight his way out of France and into Germany by way of the Rhine crossing and until the very last minutes of the war, if there was any trouble going, it was going in his vicinity.

As for his brother, that fortunate young man had been posted to Hamilton in Bermuda at an early stage and he spent a great part of the war happily there. He was demobilised six years later never, as he himself said, "having seen an angry German" in his life. The cards of chance — if that bomb in April 1942 had landed five hundred yards further along Deanston Drive our whole family would have been wiped out. But it didn't and we were alive.

If there was no dreadful outcry about the dropping of the atomic bomb, it is equally true to say that there was nothing like the mafe-king and celebrating for VJ (Victory over Japan) Day that there had been when the European conflict ended. Perhaps it was simply that it was difficult to recapture that mood of hectic abandon so soon afterwards. Perhaps it was that while the Japanese were certainly thoroughly hated, they had never been the direct personal menace to these shores that the Germans had been. Perhaps it was a realisa-tion that our problems might be beginning all over again. Certainly one or two newspapers had already noted sourly the eleventh hour and 59th minute intervention of the Soviet Union in the war against Japan, too late to be of any conceivable military use but in plenty of time to have a seat at the relevant peace conference.

There were celebrations of course, even in the comparatively muted atmosphere. On the night of VJ Day Bobby Devlin and I were walking along the banks of the Cart in Tantallon Road and we stopped to watch a group of boys who were roasting potatoes over a fire on open ground near the river-bank. No amount of eating lumpy, inedible, half-raw potatoes could convince Glaswegian boys that roasting spuds over a fire is not one of the greatest experiences of life. It was a calm, sunny evening and just beginning to darken. Suddenly, from nowhere, Bobby, a quiet reflective lad, sang two lines of a song which Dick Haymes had then made popular.

> The fire will dwindle into glowing embers,
> For we are here for such a little while.

That was all, no preamble, and it is not even the first verse of the song, nor did we normally sing songs to each other. I thought of it again, many times, a few months later when he was dead of meningitis. I grieved for him as for the footballers I had watched and who were now dead, not so much that they would miss their families but that they would not see the new players, hear the new songs, laugh at the new jokes of the radio and film stars.

It was, I suppose, fitting that the very last act of our war should be a football match. In more senses than one this was where we had come in because after the ending of the war against Germany in May, Queen's Park and Celtic had played a match at Hampden for a special trophy. A fine fast match had ended at 1-1 but Celtic were awarded the cup because they had gained the greater number of corner kicks. We thought this a most sneaky method of winning a trophy although, needless to say, had the Queen's tally of corners been greater we would have seized upon it as a most famous victory.

Now, in August, the same two clubs brought forward a league match at short notice and, oh joy!, oh rapture!, Queen's won by 2-0, thereby not only gaining victory but providing us with the chance of rubbing it in on our return to school where the great majority of our fellow pupils were Celtic supporters. As a kind of homage we made a special detour on the road home from Hampden that afternoon to pass the house in Clincart Road where our war had started and which in spirit at least we had never really left.

We had experienced much and we had learned some things. We would never quite be able to take food, light and fuel for granted because we had known the black-out, the almost invisible gas flame of the wartime cooker, the reconstituted egg and the whale meat which the Ministry of Food had done its best to push.

The country had changed in its attitude to certain fundamental things. It was much less Sabbatarian than before. The opening of municipal golf courses and bowling greens to cater for wartime munitions workers had dealt a severe blow to that and the returning ex-Servicemen who had experienced Christmas abroad would have no truck with the cold ignoring of the feast which had marked the 1930s. Although our family, being Catholic, was not in itself particularly rigid except with regard to churchgoing, my mother was always very tender of the susceptibilities of the neighbours and we were therefore forbidden to play football on Sundays, being enjoined instead to "go for a nice walk". This meant that we had either to drop the ball from the window and retrieve it on the way out, or one of us had to secrete it in his armpit while the others gave him close escort to shield what might otherwise have been taken for a gargantuan growth. Henceforth the atmosphere would be more relaxed. The bands in the Queen's Park would play such things as *Skyliner* and *Nancy with the laughing face* on Sundays.

We had started the war British and Imperial, we were ending it infinitely more Americanised. It was not only that we had heard many more American radio programmes than we would normally have done, or even perhaps seen more films. What was vastly different was that we had met actual Americans, for every second girl one heard of seemed to be awaiting clearance to rejoin boyfriend or husband in the United States. We knew a lot more about them and they knew a little more about us.

These philosophical reflections did not weigh too heavily on Philip, Frank, Bobby Devlin, Georgie Miller and myself as we played Combination on the way home from Hampden in the delightful, soft, summer afternoon sunshine and shouted the obligatory "Helluva nice!" when one or other of us did something which showed by-normal skill. I was telling myself that Queen's Park could even win the league this year and that it would be great to see such teams as Queen of the South and Ayr United again. It would be even greater to see Bill on a permanent basis again. He had written from Aberdeen saying that his father had been posted back to Glasgow, and that the family had got a house in Battlefield, within a mile of ours. No more gratifying news could possibly have signalled the end of the war. Would we be allowed to go to a game in Edinburgh? And, it might have been an effect of the light, or the angle at which I was standing, but I could swear that when I looked in the mirror this morning I had definitely been taller.